Autism & Anxiety

The Ultimate Teen Survival Guide

ISBN 9781 1 3999 8743 1

Autability offers a selection of training materials which are accredited by

The CPD Standards Authority

CPD provider: 50373

For more information on books and training materials please visit www.autability.co.uk

Other books by Charlotte Chaney & Danielle Punter

Parenting Rewired:

How to raise a happy autistic child in a very neurotypical world

ISBN 978 1 83997 072 6

Autism & Anxiety:

Learn how to support autistic children & young people overcome anxiety

ISBN 978 1 3999 5160 9

The Wonderful World of Gwen

ISBN 978 1 3999 6034 2

Foreword

Hey there! Welcome to our fourth paperback book! We're Charlotte and Danielle, and we're both authors. Like you, we are autistic, have ADHD and are dealing with anxiety.

We run a company called Autability, where we share what it's like being a kid or teen who is autistic or has ADHD (or both). We know everyone's unique and don't know what it's like to be you. What we can share, though, is what we went through at your age, as well as the most common struggles and challenges autistic and ADHD teens face.

We've written some books for parents, but this one's just for you, teenagers. If you haven't been an autistic/ADHD teen, understanding the challenges they face every day can be tricky. We all spend our teen years figuring out who we are, but for some, like those dealing with anxiety, it can feel a bit like playing a game of survival. Anxiety can make simple things feel ten times harder for us than they do for others.

You might already feel different—maybe you look different or spend all your energy trying to fit in. But inside, you're dealing with the twists and squeezes that come with anxiety. Figuring out who you are might have to wait because, for now, you are just trying to make it through each day the best you can.

This book is here to help you understand why you might feel the way you do and to give you some ideas on making daily life a bit easier. As you practice the ideas in this book, you'll free up space in your busy brain to explore who you are and what you stand for when you're ready. But that might not happen during your teenage years, and that's OK. Danielle didn't start figuring herself out until she was 21. Anxiety took over during her teen years, and her main goal was to go unnoticed (which she thinks she failed at for a long time). Charlotte started learning about who she was even later than Danielle and continues to do so daily. So, those friends who seem to have it all figured out in their teens? They don't. They just don't know it yet.

We know you're dealing with a lot right now, and hopefully, we can help with some of it. The good news is there are things you can do to lighten the load. We wish there were magic fixes, but what we do have for you are lists of ideas to get you through the day feeling as happy and calm as possible. Some days, anxiety will hit you hard. You might not see them coming, or you might be expecting it for weeks. Either way, this book aims to guide you on how to work through events so you can calm your mind and keep things in perspective. The trick is having faith in yourself to start fresh tomorrow, no matter what happened today.

It's not always about medical advice; sometimes, you need understanding from people who see life from your point of view. We genuinely hope this book helps you feel less alone and shows you how to start making small changes that will make a huge difference.

Charlotte and Danielle

Contents

INTRODUCTION

Before we start talking about how to manage anxiety, we need to chat about what anxiety is. This is because, believe it or not, not all anxiety is a bad thing.

Whether or not people realise it, everyone feels anxiety at some point in life. This is because our bodies and brains are designed to feel fear when the brain thinks that danger might be near. It puts us on a higher alert level, which sends our energy to different parts of our body and makes us faster, more alert and aware of oursurroundings. Back when man was a hunter, these bodily functions were useful and stopped us from being eaten by an animal a lot larger than we were.

Nowadays, a trip to the supermarket doesn't require the same level of "high alert" that cavemen needed when hunting for their evening meal. Over millions of years, our bodies have adapted to these changes, and most people can pop to the supermarket without using up much energy, let alone being faced with an anxiety attack. Unless you run into a grizzly bear, of course!

But what happens when our brain becomes out of sync with the world and views places that are, in fact, relatively safe as places filled with threat and danger? Yep, you guessed it, you feel anxious. An anxiety disorder is diagnosed when you view safe places or situations as a genuine danger zone. Your brain's processes take over and send your body into emergency mode, only this time, it's for the wrong reason.

So, what about those times when anxiety is a good thing? Because they do exist! The trick here is to tell the difference between a healthy nervous feeling and an anxious feeling, which causes too many physical symptoms like sweating or heavy breathing, along with a sense of panic. Many situations in life make us feel nervous. Nerves make us prepare more and give us a bit of an adrenaline kick, which can help us perform better in things like sports matches or exams. If an event means a lot to us, we will likely feel nervous, which is perfectly normal. You guys need to know when it's not normal and you need a bit of help.

Nerves become anxiety when you feel so overwhelmed or frightened that you either want to run away and hide, you respond in a way that is maybe aggressive, or you make decisions which you wouldn't do if you were calmer. This is known as Fight or Flight and means anxiety will make you run away or freeze or make you act in a way that protects you. Maybe you shout at someone you shouldn't or hide in the school toilets, hoping you won't be noticed. All of this is a survival technique that can be traced back millions of years to when man was living in the real threat of the wild, and phones were not available for you to call for help if you got into an argument with a sabre tooth tiger.

The point is, if you feel nervous about an event that means a lot to you or will affect whether you start university or get a job, that's normal. But if you feel so nervous you lose the ability to leave your bedroom, that's not so normal. And that is the type of anxiety this book is going to help you with.

But this book isn't just for anyone who is dealing with anxiety. This book is for autistic and/or ADHD teens coping with anxiety, and that brings in a whole new angle. Here's why.

Being autistic and/or having ADHD can be a real challenge, making everyday events feel anxiety-inducing, whether you have an official anxiety disorder or not. It's like running a marathon every day. Dealing with sensory stuff, planning conversations, having endless questions about why we do things, and desperately trying to fit in. We burn so much more energy to get through the day than neurotypical people could even imagine. It's tough to explain to someone who doesn't get it, and many people don't believe us because they haven't walked in our shoes.

We want you to understand that feeling anxious about small or easy tasks doesn't mean you're bad at handling daily life. We often see autistic/ADHD people feeling embarrassed that regular, everyday things can trigger anxiety. But what if we told you it's not the tasks themselves that are the problem? It's when a bunch of them pile up at the same time. Charlotte puts it like this: everyday life is like playing a game of Jenga.

If you haven't tried Jenga yet, check it out on YouTube. It's a game with a tower made of rectangular blocks stacked together. The goal is to take one block off at a time and put it on the top of the tower. You keep doing this until the bottom of the tower has too many blocks missing, and the top becomes super heavy, making the whole thing wobbly. The player who pulls out the last block before the tower crashes loses the game.

Playing Jenga might seem easy at first. The blocks look all neat and balanced, just like our daily tasks – getting dressed, going to school, doing homework, etc. Imagine each block represents a simple task. When you get dressed, you remove a block from the tower and place it on top. When you go to school, you remove a block and put it on top. And so on throughout the day.

But here's the catch: as you remove more blocks and add them to the top of the Jenga tower, it gets wobbly. Each block feels like it could be the one to make the whole thing come tumbling down.

Think of it like dealing with those everyday tasks when you have anxiety. Doing simple tasks on their own seems okay – washing your hair, leaving the house, having breakfast, or hanging out with a friend. But when you have to juggle several things simultaneously, it's like stacking those Jenga blocks. You're just waiting for that one extra thing that might make everything feel like it's falling apart.

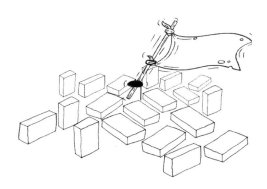

For neurotypical people, daily tasks use fewer Jenga blocks compared to autistic/ADHD people like us. So, something as simple as getting ready in the morning might only be one block for them, but it could feel like dealing with five blocks for us.

We tend to break tasks into tiny steps, pay extra attention to details, and rely on a particular routine to finish tasks without using a whole day's worth of brain power. Danielle spent most of her teenage years trying to figure out why everyone else seemed to breeze through daily life, still thinking clearly at 9 pm. By that time, Danielle's brain had checked out, and all she wanted was the peace and comfort of her bed, maybe with some fairy lights to gaze at since they felt so calming.

Being autistic and/or having ADHD comes with loads of strengths that others might be jealous of! But, like everyone else, we all face challenges, and one common hurdle for us is that everyday tasks take up more brain power than they do for others. It doesn't mean you're a failure - it just means you might need to work a bit harder than most. Sometimes, that extra effort can bring on feelings of anxiety, but don't worry, that's something we can help with.

The trick to handling anxiety is planning your activities so you don't overload yourself. It's like carefully placing each block to build a stable tower. You won't always get it perfect, and that's okay – life happens. The important part is knowing that you can gradually rebuild your tower even if things crumble. Throughout this book, we will use the Jenga tower example to show you how to keep your tower going strong for longer.

What's the difference between autism, ADHD and anxiety?

Something else you need to know from the start is the difference between how autism, ADHD and anxiety feel. It can be easy to get confused and think that a symptom of ADHD (e.g. distraction) is anxiety. To make it easier, we've popped some examples of what each diagnosis is in a table:

Autism	ADHD	Anxiety
Social Challenges: Difficulty in understanding social cues, challenges in maintaining eye contact, struggles with social interactions and relationships	Inattention: Difficulty paying attention, easily distracted, trouble organising, lots of careless mistakes	Excessive worry: Persistent, overwhelming fear about life, including future events, performance or social situations.
Repetitive behaviours: Many repetitive movements or behaviours, fixated on particular interests, sticking to strict routines or rituals.	Hyperactivity: Restlessness, excessive talking, impulsiveness, difficulty waiting for turns, fidgeting and interrupting others.	Physical Symptoms: Physical symptoms like increased heart rate, sweating, trembling, nausea, or panic attacks in response to stress or triggers.
Communication Challenges: Delayed speech or language development, difficulty in initiating or maintaining conversations, literal interpretation of language	Executive Functioning: Problems with planning, time management, prioritizing tasks, and regulating emotions.	Avoidance Behaviours: Avoiding situations or places that cause anxiety, leading to disruptions in daily life or activities.

Autism	ADHD	Anxiety
Sensory Differences: Heightened or reduced sensitivity to sensory stimuli such as light, sound, touch, taste, or smell.		

The difference between anxiety and fear

Something important to understand about anxiety is that it is different from fear. Anxiety occurs in people who are worried about the future. This includes unknown threats, so things they don't know will ever happen or be real. They have no proof that what they are worried about will happen. However, the threat is extremely real to that person, even if it never happens.

Fear is what we feel when we physically see something scary in front of us. It is a response to a known danger, something that is real right then and there in that moment. This doesn't mean anxiety is less severe or painful than fear. It is the same response, but it's in the wrong place. Your brain reacts as though it's real right then and there. But it isn't happening. Your brain is just telling your nervous system that it is.

This, again, is how anxiety is different from nerves. When you're feeling anxious, your nervous system is preparing for a severe life-threatening event, so much so that you may not be able to move, speak or eat. When you're nervous, you can still participate in daily tasks, as you just feel a bit on edge. These severe anxious reactions won't always happen straight away, but they can build up if you don't know how to stop them.

So now we know that daily life can take more effort than for many people, and what anxiety feels like, it's time to start looking at how to make different tasks and situations a bit easier for yourself. Remember, these aren't magic fixes but they are things you can actively do and take control over. Sometimes, the slightest change can give you the biggest result! So, without further ado, let's dive in!

CHAPTER 1

Morning Routine

We have all heard the expression, " I'm not a morning person." People use it when they struggle to be on time in the morning but don't have a reason other than feeling sleepy and not waking up. For most autistic/ADHD people, the morning is a challenge whether they're still feeling tired or they're wide awake.

The tasks that have to be done first thing in the morning can be a massive cause of anxiety throughout life. Some mornings can feel worse than others. As a child, Charlotte remembers feeling incredibly anxious from Sunday lunchtime onwards as the Monday morning routine approached. Monday was always worse because she knew she would also have to switch her brain back into "weekday mode," as well as the normal stresses and anxiety of the morning. It was not until many years later when she was working as a teacher and still experiencing that pre Monday morning anxiety, that she realised what she needed to do. Charlotte moved some of the tasks from Monday morning to earlier. She also realised that this could be applied to Mondays and every day of the week.

Every one of us has different things to do in the morning. We all face other challenges, too, so we can't give you a magic routine that will solve all your morning stresses (sorry!). What we can do is give you some examples of different morning structures and explain how straightforward changes can make the morning routine far less stressful and overwhelming.

Raj's morning

Morning job	Tasks & stress levels	Time & length of tasks	Difficulty/ anxiety rating
Wake up & breakfast	Raj finds waking up easy. He quickly gets out of bed and is focused on his morning routine.	Wakes up @7.00am Eats breakfast @7.15 am It takes him 15 minutes to make and eat breakfast	1/10 3/10
Personal care	Raj showers, shaves and brushes his teeth every morning. Raj gets distracted when he showers. Shaving and brushing his teeth give him energy for the day.	A shower takes up to 20 minutes as Raj finds it hard to get motivated. Raj finds shaving and brushing his teeth easy and finishes both tasks within 10 minutes.	9/10 2/10

Morning job	Tasks & stress levels	Time & length of tasks	Difficulty/ anxiety rating
Make lunch	Raj always has the same lunch. Cheese sandwiches, fruit and water. Raj finds that making lunch takes a lot of brain power, and the more stressed he becomes, the longer it takes him.	In the morning, it takes Raj 15 minutes to make a sandwich. BUT, when he gets home from school, it only takes around 1 minute. Making a sandwich isn't the problem for Raj.	9/10
Getting dressed & packing school bag	Getting clothes ready Getting dressed doesn't cause too much stress Packing bag Checking bag	Finding his clothes takes Raj a long time. He worries he doesn't have the right items. It takes 10 minutes. Getting dressed takes 5 minutes. Raj packs his bag, which takes 5 minutes He double or triple checks before school. This takes 10 minutes.	8/10 2/10 5/10 8/10

Morning job	Tasks & stress levels	Time & length of tasks	Difficulty/ anxiety rating
Travel to school/college	Raj travels to school by bike. He enjoys the ride and he has more time so he is less anxious.	Leave home by @ 8.15am. The journey takes 12-15 minutes, including pad-locking his bike at school. Registration is @ 8.30am. Raj is always running late. This makes him anxious.	7/10
		Total Time: 1 hour 55 mins	**Anxiety rating 54%**

If Raj makes a few simple changes to his morning routine, he can bring down that anxiety. Let's look at how Raj can do this by following a different routine.

Raj's Alternative Routine

Morning job	Tasks & stress levels	Time & length of tasks	Difficulty/ anxiety rating
Wake up & breakfast	Raj finds waking up easy. He quickly gets out of bed and is focused on his morning routine.	Wakes up @7.00am Eats breakfast @7.15 am It takes him 15 minutes to make and eat breakfast	1/10 3/10

Morning job	Tasks & stress levels	Time & length of tasks	Difficulty/ anxiety rating
Personal care	Raj showers in the evening now; he has a quick morning wash, which takes 5 minutes. Shaving and brushing his teeth give him energy for the day.	A quick wash takes 5 minutes. Raj finds shaving and brushing his teeth easy and finishes both tasks within 10 minutes.	2/10 2/10
Make lunch	Raj always has the same lunch. Cheese sandwiches, fruit and water. Raj finds that making lunch takes a lot of brain power, and the more stressed he becomes, the longer it takes him.	Raj makes his lunch in the evening now. In the morning, he grabs his lunch items, and it takes 5 minutes..	2/10

Morning job	Tasks & stress levels	Time & length of tasks	Difficulty/ anxiety rating
Getting dressed & packing school bag	Getting clothes ready Getting dressed doesn't cause too much stress Packing bag Checking bag	Raj gets his clothes out the night before and lays them out ready. Getting dressed takes 5 minutes. Raj packs his bag in the evening before he goes to bed. He checks it before school, which takes 5 minutes.	0/10 2/10 0/10 3/10
Travel to school/college	Raj travels to school by bike. He enjoys the ride and he has more time so he is less anxious.	Leave home by @ 8.15am. The journey takes 12-15 minutes, including padlocking his bike at school. Registration is @ 8.30am. Raj enjoys his ride to school now he has more time and is less anxious.	3/10
		Total Time: 1hr 15 mins	**Anxiety rating 18%**

By moving a few tasks to the night before, Raj not only frees up more time in the morning but also reduces the amount of brain power needed in a short amount of time in the mornings, making the tasks less daunting and less likely to build up like the Jenga tower we talked about in the introduction. Now, let's look at somebody else's morning.

Georgia's morning

Morning job	Tasks & stress levels	Time & length of tasks	Difficulty/ anxiety rating
Wake up & breakfast	Georgia finds it hard to wake up and often doesn't know what she wants for breakfast.	Wakes up @7am and is out of bed @ 7.30am She spends 15 minutes deciding what she wants for breakfast, even though she always ends up having cereal.	9/10 9/10
Personal care	She has a shower. She finds this regulating. Georgia styles her hair and puts some make up on.	Showering can take up to 15 minutes because she doesn't want it to stop. Showering calms Georgia down. She spends 15 minutes drying and styling her hair as it gets wet in the shower. Georgia spends 5 minutes putting on make up .	2/10 5/10

Morning job	Tasks & stress levels	Time & length of tasks	Difficulty/ anxiety rating
Make lunch	Georgia has lunch in the school canteen, so no tasks need to be done.	0 minutes	0/10
Getting dressed & packing school bag	Georgia gets her clothes ready.	Gerorgia gets her clothes out the night before.	1/10
	Getting dressed doesn't cause her too much stress.	Getting dressed takes 5 minutes.	2/10
	She packs her school bag.	Georgia has all her work on a laptop so it isn't too bad.	3/10
	She packs her sports bag.	Two days a week she has sports and panics she won't have the correct kit. On these days it adds an extra 15 minutes.	8/10

YOU NEED TO GET OUT OF THE SHOWER!

Morning job	Tasks & stress levels	Time & length of tasks	Difficulty/ anxiety rating
Travel to school/college	Georgia goes to school in a taxi.	The taxi is supposed to arrive between 8.30am and 8.45am but is sometimes late. Georgia worries she has been forgotten, or if she has a slow morning, she worries about keeping the taxi waiting.	9/10
		Total Time: 1hr 25 mins on non sports days. 1 hour 40 mins on sports days	**Anxiety rating 40% on non sports days and 48% on sports days**

Let's look at ways Georgia can make her morning less stressful.

Georgia's Alternative Routine

Morning job	Tasks & stress levels	Time & length of tasks	Difficulty/ anxiety rating
Wake up & breakfast	Georgia finds it hard to wake up and often doesn't know what she wants for breakfast. Georgia now has her own cupboard, with just her breakfast cereal in. This makes it much easier for her to wake up as she is less overwhelmed by breakfast choices.	Wakes up @7am and is out of bed @ 7.15am she can now take 15 minutes to eat breakfast and enjoy it	5/10 3/10
Personal care	She has a shower. She finds this regulating. Georgia styles her hair and puts some make up on.	Showering can take up to 15 minutes because she doesn't want it to stop. It calms Georgia down. Georgia now wears a shower cap so just needs to quickly brush her hair. Georgia spends 5 minutes putting on make up .	2/10 2/10

Morning job	Tasks & stress levels	Time & length of tasks	Difficulty/ anxiety rating
Make lunch	Georgia has lunch in the school canteen, so no tasks need to be done.	0 minutes	0/10
Getting dressed & packing school bag	Georgia gets her clothes ready. Getting dressed doesn't cause her too much stress. She packs her school bag. She packs her sports bag.	Georgia gets her clothes out the night before. Getting dressed takes 5 minutes. Georgia has all her work on a laptop so it isn't too bad. Georgia now packs her sports bag the night before.	1/10 2/10 3/10 2/10

Morning job	Tasks & stress levels	Time & length of tasks	Difficulty/ anxiety rating
Travel to school/college	Georgia goes to school in a taxi.	The taxi is supposed to arrive between 8.30 am and 8.45 am but is sometimes late. The taxi drivers now text her Mum when they leave the previous house. Georgia is less stressed and sometimes has time for a game on her console, which regulates her.	4/10
		Total Time: 55 mins on non sports days and sports days	**Anxiety rating 22% on non sports days and 24% on sports days**

As you can see from these examples, we haven't been able to remove the anxiety around morning routines altogether, but we have managed to reduce it a lot by making some minor changes. The alternative routines show how much time can be freed up in a morning, meaning that every second doesn't count in the stressful preparation for school, learning or work. It also shows how we all find different things challenging and that there is no shame in that. Georgia and Raj have helped themselves to find ways of reducing their anxiety, and that is a great way to boost their self-esteem.

When you're a morning person

In both our examples, we have shown how doing some of the morning routine tasks the night before has been an enormous help in reducing morning stress. Some people, though, can struggle to do any tasks in the evening, as they are so exhausted from the day. Their Jenga tower has fallen over, and they have nothing left to start rebuilding it until they have had enough sleep or rest so that their brain and executive function are back up and working again.

For people who are far more alert in the mornings, the answer can often be to use the evening time to relax and leave jobs until the morning if they can. What this does mean is that to be able to reduce your anxiety, you may need to get up earlier. It's not always about being prepared the night before, it can be about giving yourself plenty of time in the morning.

Danielle has always been an early riser since primary school. She found the morning rush so overwhelming that she asked for her own alarm clock when she was around 8 years old. She got up before anyone else and took a 10 to 15-minute rest between tasks. As she got older and more tasks were added to her morning schedule, the rests between tasks became shorter, but Danielle always made time to sit and watch at least 15 minutes of morning TV to allow her brain to regulate.

As an adult, the morning dog walk is an excellent way of finding time for some quiet before the chaos of the morning school run. If Danielle doesn't walk the dog, she doesn't find the morning routine any less stressful, even with the extra time she has. This is because of the noise and movement of others in the house, or she sleeps a little more and is thrown out of routine.

Only you know which tasks you can do the night before, if

any. Reducing morning anxiety is different for everyone and doesn't work if you end up making yourself more anxious the night before instead.

Preparing the night before doesn't always make it less stressful the next morning.

As we said in the introduction, the key is to space out your tasks where you can, giving yourself enough time to rebuild your Jenga tower, or recharge your brain so that you can think clearly and calmly.

CHAPTER 2

Transitions

Going through significant changes can be tough, especially for autistic teens. Examples include when you switch schools or start a new job. These changes can make us anxious because our brains have a hard time adjusting to new routines, places, or what's expected of us. Even after the change is over, the anxiety doesn't just go away. It can stick around and even worsen as we undergo more changes. So yes, transitions can be pretty tricky for us.

There are many different types of transitions, such as:

• Physical transitions: When you move physically from one place to another, e.g. home to school, classroom to playground, etc.

• Transitions between activities, e.g. different lessons at school or moving from watching TV to eating dinner.

• Transitions between roles, e.g. from being a pupil talking to teachers to being a son or daughter talking to your parent or carer at home.

It is always important to try and understand why something can make you anxious, as this helps you to learn about your autistic profile. How anxiety impacts you is the first step to understanding how you can take further steps to help yourself. Let's look at a few areas of transitions that can be a bit of a challenge.

Whether we like it or not, a transition involves some change. Changing can be hard, especially when you want things to be predictable and routine. When faced with something new, it can make you feel scared and worried because you're unsure what will happen next. When there's a change, it can feel like everything's getting messed up. It's like losing something familiar, which leaves you feeling all mixed up and out of sorts. This dislike of change can show up as anxious behaviour, meltdowns, pulling away from things, or even acting out as you try to feel more in control when everything feels chaotic.

Change usually means uncertainty. As we said in the introduction, anxiety is a fear of what might happen. When things are uncertain, there are usually lots of different situations that could occur. You can feel anxious over more than one scenario, and this is why uncertainty often makes anxiety worse. Uncertainty means you don't know what will happen, what things could go wrong or what unexpected stuff you will have to deal with. This makes the whole transition even more stressful for you.

As well as disliking uncertainty, lots of autistic people are extra sensitive to things like sounds, textures, and lights. When you move from one place to another, you might encounter new things that your senses aren't used to, like different sounds or bright lights. This can make you feel uncomfortable and overwhelmed, especially when you're going from the calm of home to the busy school noise. It can make you feel like you are physically in pain and mentally overloaded, which increases your stress levels.

Routine changes can feel scary and overwhelming, making us want to just stay at home.

Then, you have the social side of transitions. Making your way through social situations can be a real challenge for autistic people, and transitions usually mean dealing with new social scenarios of some kind. Maybe you're starting at a new school, joining a different club, or moving between classes. These changes can throw you into social situations you're not used to, making you feel exposed and worried. You might be scared of being left out, teased, or not understood, which can make your transition anxiety even worse. Sometimes, you might even start avoiding social stuff or keeping to yourself more because of it.

Try to remember that any change in transition is temporary. If a transition is going to change, it's usually either for a long time or just once due to a change in circumstances. Try not to panic (although we know it's easier said than done), as soon the regular routine will return, or you will adjust.

No, it doesn't always feel pleasant, but everyone has times when things are hard for them. It's about trying your best and being aware of your own needs. For example, if you need as much warning as possible before a transition, let your school or boss know.

Executive functioning

To transition from one thing to another, whatever it may be, you need to use your executive functioning. Executive functioning is what we use to describe your thinking skills like planning, organising, and finishing things, which are important for handling transitions well.

Using our executive functioning to work out the changes needed for a different transition can be overwhelming and exhausting.

But lots of autistic people find these skills challenging. It can be hard to prepare for and adjust to changes smoothly when you struggle with managing time, figuring out what's most important, and solving problems. These challenges can make transition times feel overwhelming and stressful as you try to deal with everything that's changing.

One of the biggest changes in transition is time. It's not just about the transition itself; it's about being allowed time to regulate after you have done the actual transition. Charlotte's autistic son is 18, and he struggles with transitions, particularly those that involve people. He needs time to get used to having a new person with him. If he is given enough time to do this, then he manages to keep his anxiety at bay. But if someone expects him to engage with a new person he doesn't know immediately, he quickly becomes too anxious, leading to a meltdown.

Regulation time can also be created, which you can schedule into your day. When Charlotte was a teacher, she found the transitions of the school day just as challenging as she did when she was a pupil. She knew that there wouldn't be the opportunity to have time to calm down and regulate her senses between each lesson period. Instead, she would schedule them into her day.

The quickest way for Charlotte to get to work was by bus, a train, and another bus. A sensory nightmare! What she did was walk instead of catching the bus. This walking was a lifesaver. On her way to work, she would listen to music and be alone with her thoughts, preparing herself for the transitions of the day ahead. On her way home, she would prepare for the transition back home but also think about and release the stress from the transitions she had gone through during the day. This time was essential for Charlotte. Yes, it added about two hours to the length of her day, but the benefit to her well-being was enormous.

Danielle handles her transitions slightly differently from Charlotte. She also plans times into her day to regulate and calm, but they are much shorter. Danielle is always early for everything for two reasons. First, she worries about her time management as she struggles to predict how long tasks will take. When late, her anxiety gets worse, and her executive functioning completely fails. She can't think, she can't plan, she can't pick out clothes, etc. Anxiety seems to wipe out the executive function Danielle has. Why? Because being late is one of the main fears Danielle has about transitions and so anxiety has more power over her when she is running late. This is something Danielle learned about herself at quite a young age, and being early for everything, while sometimes being a pain, eased that anxiety and meant her executive functioning worked better.

The second is because she needs time to let her brain leave one activity or place and transition to the next activity or place before she goes into an appointment or building. Just like Charlotte needed her walks, for Danielle, sitting quietly for 10 minutes lets her thoughts settle and stop racing, which lessens anxiety. So even though Danielle has ADHD, which impacts her daily life quite severely, she is early and not late like people seem to assume those with ADHD will be. It helps with the stress of transitions, right down to simply doing the school run with her son.

Danielle was always early for lessons at school, but not because she wanted to look like a model student. The mental pain of being late would turn to physical pain if the anxiety became too bad, especially when it came to noise, which blocks even more of her brain power when anxious. Ease that anxiety how you need to, and you can help yourself to have more energy throughout the day, too!

Why "good" transitions can sometimes be bad

One massive misconception about transitions is that they are either "good" or "bad", and "good" transitions are not stressful. This is NOT the case! Several transitions Charlotte and Danielle go through each day would be considered "good".

Charlotte's favourite transition of the day is putting pyjamas on. She finds them the most comfortable thing she wears, and when she has them on, her body almost breathes a sigh of relief. However, that doesn't mean transitioning from daytime to nighttime clothing isn't stressful. To get relief from pyjamas, Charlotte must process the motor planning of getting clothes off, hanging them up, or putting them in the laundry basket. She feels the temperature change, so she has to choose the pyjamas and use motor planning for her muscles to put the pyjamas on physically.

After this, Charlotte will spend a few minutes regulating the transition before continuing with the next part of her routine. If the transition involves other stresses, such as a time limit, it will make it more complicated, but remember, there is no shame in finding the nicer transitions hard.

Danielle adores the transition of putting make-up on in the morning because it is like artwork to her. But when it goes wrong, it feels hugely stressful because of time limits and a disruption to routine. Suddenly, one of the best transitions of the day becomes the worst. And that's OK. You can bounce back from these things by thinking about how others can help give you more time (they could find your school bag while you catch up with your routine) and whether there are parts of your routine that perhaps you could skip that day to help give you more time.

The transition to school

Charlotte once taught a young person who struggled with the transition into school, like many of you and us. There was a lot of understanding around this from school and home because it was common knowledge why autistic children/teens found the move from home to school so hard. What wasn't understood was why they went through the same problems when transitioning from school to home. Why would going home to your favourite place cause such difficulties? It wasn't home that was the problem, but the stress from the day which had built up for the young person, and getting home when the brain had already been through so much.

The physical, environmental and sensory changes during a transition to school or work and back can be huge. Some examples include:

- Leaving the environment of the house and being faced by the weather. It could be going from warm to cold, dry to wet, calm to windy. You could have been in your house waiting to leave, too hot as you're wearing a coat inside. Suddenly, your coat isn't warm enough.

- Using public transport, which requires a lot of planning, including the conversations needed to buy tickets etc.

- The noises, the smells and just general sensory stuff that you're not in control of. It can be overloading, and it's not like you can just ask people on the bus to talk more quietly or take a shower!

- Moving from the role of family member to student. Your language and behaviour with a different set of adults has to change completely, and you have to constantly remember where you are so you act the right way. The last thing you want is to call your teacher "Mum"… Oh, the embarrassment!

The different sensory inputs you face on the way to school can mean it's even harder for you to manage the sensory environment in the classroom.

We reckon that at least one home-to-school transition challenge will be familiar to you. You may even think that if so many things make transitions difficult, it is a bit of a lost cause and not even worth trying. Yes, transitions can be difficult and yes, there may be lots of different parts you struggle with. BUT! For each part of a transition that causes anxiety, there are several ways to make this easier for you. The more parts you make easier for yourself, the less stress you will feel!

How to make transitions easier for yourself

How to make transitions easier for yourself varies from person to person. Sometimes, you might feel you need to limit how many changes you go through daily. But that might not make life as good as it could be in the long term. Reducing your transitions for a shorter temporary time to help you recover from burnout, though, would be very helpful.

Here are some ideas to get you started with making your transitions easier:

1. *Learn what you struggle with the most*

Knowing what makes transitions challenging is the first step to easing some of the anxiety and stress they bring. It's important not to feel ashamed of these feelings because they're unique to you. Maybe keep a diary or score the transitions throughout your day out of ten, one being easy and ten being the most difficult. Perhaps the transition home is quick because you're desperate to get there, but how do you feel at home? Did you give yourself time to de-stress? Spend a week or so making a few notes for yourself. You need to know you to make this easier.

2. *Move tasks to a different time of day*

Switch up the order you do stuff. As discussed in Chapter One, if taking a shower and washing your hair is hard, maybe do it when you're not about to head off to school. Just taking a shower involves many changes, so spreading these tasks out at different times of the day and giving yourself more time to recover might make things easier.

3. *Use a transition object*

Try to keep something the same by using a transition

object. When you were a kid, maybe you had a special toy or something that helped you feel more secure during transitions. Well, guess what? Grown-ups can use them too! It's like a tool to keep something familiar with you. And it doesn't have to be the same every day, just something that stays the same. Like in the winter, Charlotte will often wear a scarf. It feels cosy and safe, especially when she sprays it with calming essential oils. So, not only does it give her a familiar smell, but if she becomes overwhelmed Charlotte can smell her scarf to help calm down. It doesn't have to be clothes, either. It could be a water bottle, a pen, or a keychain. Whatever it is, you can focus on it throughout the day.

4. *Make some transitions longer*

Make some transitions longer so you have time to calm down and feel more regulated. You might think that the faster you can complete a transition, the less painful it will be. For some people that might be true, but for others a fast transition can make things a whole lot worse. Like Charlotte's example of walking instead of catching the bus, if you think extra time is needed to listen to music and be with your thoughts before you get to school/work or home, do it! The idea of it might be exhausting, but sometimes, being a little physically tired can help your mind clear of anxiety, leaving you with more energy!

5. *Find just a few minutes quiet*

Create a few minutes of quiet before starting a new lesson or returning to work from your break. Sometimes, if the sensory side of things allows, Danielle has found that just a few minutes of quiet in the toilets or outside to calm her mind helped when the onslaught of the classroom or work environment was about to hit. It's like emptying your brain of any noise so that there is room to cope with extra when you head back to a crowded area. Even when you're with friends you feel most comfortable with, there is still conversation and noise, etc., which, as positive as this can be, adds to the build-up before a transition.

There are a lot of transitions people don't think about, but if you take the time to think about them, you can make your life so much easier!

CHAPTER 3
Clothing, Uniforms and Outfits

Ah, the world of clothing anxiety. It's like a two-for-the-price-of-one offer. Part of it is how our brains are wired, especially for those of us with autistic differences, and part of it is tied to self-esteem and the desire to fit in.

You might be thinking, "How can clothes cause anxiety?" If your clothes are uncomfortable, you won't feel at ease. And if you're already dealing with general anxiety, it just adds to the mix.

Imagine squirming in your school uniform. You manage to tolerate it, but it's like a wrestling match that drains your energy. This struggle could mean you miss something in class, draw attention to your fidgeting, or can't focus on what you should be doing. See how it all weaves together to create more anxiety?

For those who haven't experienced anxiety, it can be a bit tricky to grasp how seemingly small things can trigger a whirlwind in your mind. If you're neurotypical, understanding the daily sensory overload we feel might be a puzzle too. Anxiety and sensory overload together can be the perfect combination for standing out in the crowd. We've got some practical tips to help you stay comfortable and focused, which will hopefully boost your confidence, too.

Let's talk about ideas for mastering the art of dealing with clothes!

When our clothes are uncomfortable, it can be challenging to concentrate on anything else. The feeling of the clothes is over-powering!

1. Comfortable materials

Choose materials that treat your skin right. Think soft cotton, tag-less gear, and textures that feel nice and comfortable against your skin.

2. Gradual exposure

Got a new job with a uniform? Take it slowly, introducing each piece of clothing one at a time. Once you've conquered one, add another – you've got this.

3. *Planning*

Going to a big event? Plan your outfit in advance to ease the anxiety. Try it on and make sure the feel of that dress or shirt won't ruin you wherever you're heading. Wear it around your room a few times and give the FULL outfit a dress rehearsal. Even for regular days, pick your clothes the night before – one less thing to stress about in the morning.

4. *Sensory integration techniques*

Before diving into new clothes, prep your senses. Sensory integration is all about waking up your body in the right way and getting used to the feel of different textures. Just like athletes warm up for a race, warm up before you know you have to wear clothes that cause discomfort or are different from your usual outfits. Try brushing your skin with a body brush or deep pressure with weighted blankets to keep your sensory game strong. Even simple stretches or body lotions or creams can help. They all get your skin used to feeling without sending it into sensory shock.

5. *Modify clothing*

Lose the tags, cut out those annoying seams, and explore adaptive items made for ultimate sensory comfort. It might seem like a small step, but it is worth it. Don't think that removing tags or flyaway pieces of thread won't make much of a difference. It only takes a few minutes, and the result can be the key between enjoying your trip or being distracted the entire time, missing out on being focused on why you're there.

6. *Routine and predictability*

Set a dressing routine. Predictability gives you a sense

of control. Your brain will thank you for it. For the daily dress, put clothes on in a certain order at a particular time. After a while, your brain and body will prepare for it subconsciously, and it will take far less of a toll on your energy and anxiety levels.

7. *Building confidence*

Your style, your rules. Some folks don't care about what they wear, and that's fine. Others have their signature choices. There's no right or wrong. Go with whatever makes you feel comfy and confident.

8. *Asking for help*

Don't hesitate to reach out for advice. Picking the right outfit or understanding dress codes can be tricky. Having a trusted friend or family member can ease the anxiety, from pre-event nerves to the actual outing.

Remember, what works varies from person to person. Trial and error is the game here. Your brain's sensory processing isn't a robot – it's unique. Embrace it, manage those feelings, and conquer that anxiety.

Uniforms

Whether for school or work, you can't magically change how uniforms feel. But you can distract yourself and ramp up your comfort level. Here are our ideas to make those uniform days more bearable:

1. *Soft layers*

Pop on a soft vest or a T-shirt under your school shirt. Go for white so it doesn't stand out. Feeling that soft touch against your skin instead of the scratchy shirt can bring total relief and give you more brain space to focus on what's happening around you.

2. *Comfy feet*

Soft socks and memory foam insoles are brilliant for helping prevent brain overload from pain. The comfort makes all the difference, especially if you struggle to tolerate the style of shoes you have to wear. Sadly, we can't go to school in our slippers. We wish!

3. *Tie tricks*

Got to wear a tie? Practice the knot, but keep it loose enough to cover your top button when it's undone.

4. *Light-reactive lenses*

Sunglasses might be a no-go in school or your weekend job, but lenses that react to light and tint in bright surroundings can be a game changer. Those bright classroom lights can be dulled without changing your glasses, and the sunlight streaming into the room can be dimmed. Make sure you try out any lenses at a proper optician before you buy; you need them to react quickly enough!

5. *Use your favourite scents*

Drown out those not-so-great sensations by going heavy on your favourite body spray or perfume. Trust us, it works better than you'd think! For an extended smell, spray your clothes. The scent will hang around longer. There are also pendants and jewellery (if allowed) that you can put essential oils into, and they will help when you need a calming scent to bring you back from the brink of overload.

6. *Hand cream magic*

Smooth and nice-smelling hands can help. It gives your brain something else to focus on. A pleasant, calming sensation of putting on hand cream, with a scent that distracts from your surroundings, can help regulate you in moments of stress or overload.

7. *Winter warmth with scarves*

For the chilly months, embrace large, soft scarves. They're like a cosy hug and a sensory pillow for your head when it's hurting. Plus, they give you that feeling of being a bit more incognito.

These ideas have been tested by those who get it. Give them a go and see what works for you!

Navigating the Style Struggle

Understanding fashion can be an actual anxiety trigger, especially for autistic/ADHD teens. We've all been there – showing up at a social event wearing a completely different style or mismatched outfit. Take Danielle, for instance; back in her early secondary school days, she rocked up to a sponsored walk in woodland and muddy fields wearing clothes worthy of clubbing, definitely not the right choice of outfit!

Back in her school "dress-up" days, like career days, she refused to squeeze into uncomfortable heels at age 13. Doc Martens and walking boots were her go-to choices. Danielle embraced the confidence to wear whatever she wanted as she got older. Her anxiety about fashion came from not wanting to stand out. Nowadays, with the internet at her fingertips, she looks online at fashion options and learns how to pair comfy items with the latest trends. Now in her

40s, Danielle swears by the calming effect of knowledge. Online browsing for the perfect combination of comfort and style is her primary way of keeping her anxiety under control. Knowledge is the key. You'll be surprised at the stylish and calming outfits you can create when you see a few examples for yourself.

If fashion rules aren't your thing, who cares? Express yourself! Sometimes, being the odd one out is a badge of honour. Anxiety can just as quickly fade by just being yourself. Embrace your style, be proud, and tackle those worries head-on. For many, this self-empowerment is the ultimate calm within.

CHAPTER 4

Overload in the Classroom

School can be challenging for autistic people, even for autistic teachers and teaching assistants. Sights, sounds and smells can stop your brain from working and make it hard to think.

Learning how to handle your surroundings becomes more important as you grow older. As you learn more about your autism, you'll find ways to deal with things that make you anxious. Here are a few general ideas to help you start thinking about the classroom.

1. *Where to sit in class*

The environment is crucial. Some things, like how the room is set up and the lighting, you can't change. But if something would help you feel better, it's OK to ask for it, either by talking directly to or through a trusted adult. For example, you might ask to sit in a particular spot to avoid bright lights or distracting decorations. Where you sit can make a big difference in hearing the teacher and not feeling overwhelmed by others.

2. *Try to be tidy*

Keeping things tidy can make things easier for you. Ensure you have the right tools for your class, but don't bring too much stuff. For instance, you wouldn't need math tools during an English lesson.

Too much equipment can make you feel flustered, so only have out what you need for the lesson.

3. Feel in control

Visual schedules or timers can help you know what's coming next and remind you how your day is planned. This will help you feel more organised and in control. These tools don't have to be fancy; you could use a notebook to write down your schedule or put a timetable on your laptop or phone.

4. Short breaks to recharge

Asking for breaks is an excellent way to stay calm and

avoid feeling too stressed. Danielle did this a lot in school by offering to run errands. It gave her a break from the classroom when she needed to move around or have a sensory break. If you think you'd feel better with a short break to move around or change your surroundings, it's wise to have a plan. This way, all your teachers know about it, and you don't have to ask for a break when you're feeling overwhelmed.

5. *Quiet fidget toys*

Classrooms can get noisy, even if everyone's quiet. With so many people around, there are always unexpected sounds. You can try using quiet fidget toys like stress balls, putty, or small toys to help yourself stay focused without bothering anyone else. Also, practising deep breathing can help you feel calmer when anxious or overwhelmed.

6. *Find a trusted adult or friend*

Finding a way to talk to staff about how you're feeling and what you need is helpful. You don't have to speak out loud if you're uncomfortable – there are other ways to communicate. Don't be afraid to ask for changes that would help you. Things can usually be adjusted to fit your needs, so don't settle for something that doesn't feel right.

If you feel like it, you can tell close friends about your diagnosis and teach them about autism and sensory issues. This can help them support you better and make you feel more included and understood.

The classroom may seem like a world of sensory overload, but when you take all the small things you can change, it can become much more manageable and less anxiety-inducing.

CHAPTER 5

School and Work Break Times

Breaks and unstructured times can make autistic people feel anxious. A structure gives us a sense of predictability, making us feel safe. As you grow older and get through high school and beyond, you'll find that the world allows you to use break times however you like. Most people enjoy this freedom, but many autistic/ADHD people find the free time causes them anxiety. There are many options for what to do with your time, meaning you must make decisions. Making decisions can make us feel tired and stressed if we take too long to decide. When we are younger, adults guide us through break times or free time, so we don't have to use as much energy thinking about what to do.

In primary school, more teachers usually organise play and activities during break times. There's less guidance in secondary school and college, which can be more stressful. The good news is that there are ways to make these times more manageable. Here are some ideas.

1. *Find a safe space*

Look for, or make, a safe place in the school where you can feel calm and relaxed. It could be a quiet spot in the library, the pastoral care department, or a classroom. Talk to your school about needing a safe space; they can help find a good spot for you.

---

2. *Plan ahead*

Plan some activities and maybe make a list of hobbies that you can enjoy during break time. Having a plan or something enjoyable can reduce anxiety before, during and after the break time.

3. *Cut out the noise*

Try using noise-cancelling headphones or earplugs to manage the sensory environment around you. They're less noticeable than ear defenders, so others might not even realise. Also, consider having a little kit with sensory tools like fidget toys, stress balls, or textures that help you feel calm and in control.

4. *Find others like you*

Build a group of friends who understand and make you feel at ease during breaks. Having someone to chat with or hang out with can give you a feeling of safety and make time pass faster.

Finding others who need the same things as you at break times can help you feel more supported.

5. *Make up your own routine*

Planning ahead for what you'll do during break can also be a helpful way to lessen anxiety. Even though breaks are usually free time, adding some structure by creating your routines is OK. This could include having a snack at a particular time, taking a short walk, spending time with friends or doing an activity.

Remember, working on skills to help yourself through break times doesn't only happen during break times. You can practice at home before or after you find yourself in a situation that makes you anxious. You could try relaxation techniques, like deep breathing, to handle anxiety when break times get tough. Working on social skills can help, too, by practising role-playing or getting advice from a trusted adult.

Remember, it's all about discovering what works best for you. Try different approaches, be patient with yourself, and know that managing anxiety during school breaks will take time. Some days will be easier than others, and that's OK. The important thing is that you're taking steps to manage your anxiety.

CHAPTER 6

School Free Time

Teens and children who think and learn differently can find going to school hard. Lately, more people have noticed this, and it's even been talked about in TV news, on shows, and online. But there's something else: not many people talk about how these young people feel after school is over for the day or during the school holidays. This can be challenging for those who get nervous about school and those who usually don't. This chapter will examine why we might feel anxious when not in school and how we can lower our anxiety during these times.

After school

Charlotte liked school, and even though it was far from easy for her, in her mind, it offered a routine and structure that calmed her brain, even though there were complex challenges that came with it. In junior school, after school was a time that left her feeling anxious as her time lacked routine and structure. This improved slightly in secondary school as Charlotte had music lessons or rehearsals most days after school, giving her the structure she craved.

We often hear that demands can cause anxiety, which we know for some autistic people is true (see "Demands and Requests" chapter), but the way an autistic brain works means we like things to be in order. This helps us not feel so worried about what we need to do. But finding the right balance is hard. We need time to chill, think about things, and get over the day. Yet, we don't want too much free time where we end up putting things off and feeling anxious about what happened today or what could happen tomorrow.

Another cause of anxiety after school can be being encouraged to "hang out" with friends and peers. This can be great fun! But it can mean that you are doing things you don't think are the best idea, or you get in trouble with parents/carers because you are not home at the expected time. When she was 11, Danielle can remember being invited out by a group of girls on Halloween. She had just started secondary school, and whilst she wasn't worried about seeing them socially, she was worried that her Mum had given her strict rules not to go trick or treating. She knew the others wanted to go and was torn over what to do. The anxiety of breaking her Mum's rules took over her head, yet all she wanted to do was fit in with those her age. Ultimately, she went trick or treating but barely registered what was happening because she was so anxious about her Mum finding out that she spent the whole evening in a daze and on the verge of overload. And yes, her Mum did find out because Danielle was, and still is, a terrible liar!

We've got lots of things that you can try to help with this time of day. As with all the ideas in this book, you will find things that work and help a lot and things that make little or no difference for you. So, where do you start?

Firstly, you need to understand two critical things. These are what you NEED after school and what you NEED to make yourself less anxious. To work this out, try asking yourself these questions:

1. What do you NEED to do after school to regulate and

recover after a day at school?

2. What do you HAVE to do after school? This could include homework, household chores or attending clubs or activities.

3. What do you WANT to do after school?

Your answers might look something like this:

Example 1

	NEED to	**HAVE to**	**WANT to**
Monday	Rest and play video games	Homework, Empty the dishwasher	Watch TV, Meet friends at the park
Tuesday	Rest and play video games	Homework, help to cook dinner	Go to a friend's house
Wednesday	Rest and play video games	Homework, band practice	Go to a cafe with friends
Thursday	Rest and play video games	Homework, load the dish-washer	Go to a friend's house
Friday	Rest and play video games	Homework, youth club	Go out for pizza with friends before youth club

Or it might look like this:

Example 2

	NEED to do	HAVE to do	WANT to do	COULD do
Monday	Rest	Homework	Nothing	Visit family, Baking
Tuesday	Rest	Homework, extra tuition	Nothing	Walk the dog, Go to a cafe with your parent/carer
Wednes-day	Rest	Homework	Nothing	Go to the cinema
Thurs-day	Rest	Swimming club	Nothing	Go bowling with friends
Friday	Rest	Homework	Nothing	Youth club

These two examples show opposite problems that most likely have the same cause.

In the first example, the person knows they must rest and regulate with video games. They know they must do set things on set days but want to do many other things. In the second example, the person also knows what they need to and must do but has reached a point where they don't want to do anything, even though they could.

What both examples need is a compromise. We know this is easier said than done, but working towards that mindset will help you in the short and long term. For every teenager, these years allow you to move from childhood to adulthood. Skills such as adapting to changes, compromising on things and learning to plan your time effectively can be the difference between surviving and thriving in adult life! Do you want to scrape by each day just about surviving this world? Or take the world by storm and experience amazing things! Learning to compromise could make all the difference.

Deciding between rest and other activities is not always an easy compromise.

A compromise plan for example one could look like this:

Example 1

Monday	Rest Homework Play video games Empty dishwasher Watch TV	They haven't met with friends as they don't want to start the week by making themselves more tired.
Tuesday	Go to a friend's house to do homework Rest Help cook dinner Play video games	You have combined going to a friend's house with doing homework.
Wednesday	Rest Homework Band practice Play video games	Band practice is social, so you can skip the cafe this time.
Thursday	Rest play video games Homework Load dishwasher	You've been out the last two nights, so a night in will help you stay regulated.
Friday	Rest Homework Pizza Youth Club	As it's the weekend you have an extra social activity because you can rest more over the weekend.

In example one, the focus was on removing some of the activities. One way we can deal with anxiety is to not over-commit and do too much. This can be so hard, especially when you're feeling good! You forget what your mind and body need, and before you know it, you've said yes to all sorts of events and activities, which, if not managed, ends you back at square one with a very anxious mindset.

Example two is someone who has become withdrawn and lost their motivation. With this example, we need to balance not doing enough and doing too much.

Example 2

Monday	Rest Homework	Not adding anything on Monday as it might be overwhelming due to transitioning from the weekend to the school week
Tuesday	Rest Homework Dog walk Extra tuition	A dog walk is good physical exercise, which helps with anxiety and school/tuition.
Wednesday	Rest Homework Baking	Baking can be fun and boost self-esteem when you create something delicious!
Thursday	Rest Homework Swimming	Thursdays are already busy with swimming, so you don't need to add anything.
Friday	Rest Homework Meet friends for a birthday party	You might find it hard to attend a friend's birthday party, but they will be glad you made the effort. You could stay for a short while, which would be more manageable.

Without a doubt, after school is an essential time for you to be able to regulate, relax and have control, especially when the rest of the day is incredibly structured and fast-moving. If you find that the after-school time is a period where you are not motivated to do anything, try to view this time as "your time" rather than "free time". The reason for this is that free time implies you don't have to do anything, and this can and does make people feel more anxious.

Too much free time, especially when we are tired and need regulation, is not always a good thing. Free time allows us to reset and is essential; however, it is also a time when our brilliant brains can start to think about things that have happened during the day or panic about things that might happen tomorrow.

What does help is structure. By this, we mean things to do. If it helps to process your day by talking to people, then having a time slot in the evening to talk through things with an adult at home is excellent. Sometimes, having time to "sit and talk" can be daunting, but combining it with an activity such as cooking, walking a dog or playing a game in the garden gets your mind active and reduces your focus on what you're talking about.

Sitting around doing nothing often makes anxiety worse. Thoughts go around in your head and usually build up to be worse than anything you are worried about. Distraction can be a great way to reduce anxiety.

School Holidays

School holidays are like Marmite - you either love or hate them and probably hold extreme views. School holidays can help with anxiety, and they can also make it worse. Let's take a look at the pros and cons and see how you can keep your anxiety to a minimum.

Positive points	Negative points
Time to rest and relax	Free time can mean you feel anxious
Time to do things you want to	Change in routine and transitions
Time to learn new things	Places are busier
Time to catch up on outstanding work	Boredom

- *Time to rest and relax*

You might find that during the first few days of school holidays, you struggle to do much, if anything at all. This is fine. Allow your body and brain to recover from the school term. It gives you the chance to recharge your batteries fully. This can help to reduce anxiety as rest, especially sleep, can regulate stress hormones such as cortisol. When you rest, your cortisol levels are more stable, which lowers anxiety.

Rest also helps with emotional regulation; you're less likely to have mood swings or sudden reactions you don't control. If you have a stable mood, you can stay calmer when faced with situations that usually make you anxious.

- *Time to do things you want to*

Doing things you enjoy is a brilliant way to reduce anxiety. They give you a focus, distracting you and stopping you from overthinking. Familiar activities can help you feel safe and settled, as they don't require as much mental energy. Then, you don't feel exhausted and worn out mentally at the end of the day, and it encourages better sleep, too.

- *Time to learn new things*

Learning in the holidays might seem strange, as it is the school holidays after all! But, if you have a brain that craves information and loves to learn new facts, learning about the things you CHOOSE to learn about in the holidays could be a great way to stay calm, happy and occupied.

When Charlotte was a teenager, she was (and still is) a musician, and the holidays gave her time away from schoolwork to practice her musical skills.

One summer, she decided to teach herself a new instrument and challenge herself to take an exam the following term. She hired a clarinet and spent the summer learning this new skill. This gave Charlotte a focus and a way to cope with the change from school to holiday mode.

- *Catch up on missed work*

We appreciate that using your holidays to catch up on schoolwork doesn't sound fun. But it can be a great way to lower your anxiety. Whether you've missed lessons or need extra time to take on any learning, setting aside small slots to do school work can help reduce the stress around being behind with lessons.

Doing some school work also has the added benefit of keeping the structure of your days similar between school days and holiday days. It can make it easier to manage that transition from being a full-time pupil to being a full-time family member temporarily.

Don't underestimate the impact of feeling confident in understanding your school work. It can lower your anxiety levels!

As usual, when something brings a lot of positives, it usually brings some challenges, too. Let's take a look at how the holidays can worsen our anxiety and what we can do to manage that.

• *Time for worrying*

Free time isn't always thought about as a bad thing, but when you're struggling with anxiety, it absolutely can be. When you're in the routine of a busy term, there isn't always time to worry, which is a good thing. Some of us will always find time to worry, but for many, being busy is the best way to distract themselves.

The free time of the school holidays means we have more time to worry about things. When we worry, we often think about the events or circumstances that have caused us to feel anxious. This can be positive as long as you're thinking about things in a calm and structured way. Ways to do this include asking yourself some set questions or giving yourself time to think about it before stopping and distracting yourself for a while. You can always revisit your thoughts later.

• *Swapping "modes"*

Many believe the most significant transition occurs during term time when you go from home to school and to each lesson or activity. Whilst this is true, it is not unusual for autistic people to have "modes" which they transition between.

Many of us have a "term time mode" and a "holiday mode". These modes have different places we visit, clothes we wear, foods we eat and people we spend time with. The transition between these two modes can be hugely exhausting! The build-up towards the start of the holidays and the beginning of term is a common cause of anxiety, too, as you prepare for this vast transition once again. Give yourself time to adjust and prepare for these changes.

How difficult it is to find a new mode of living will depend on how much you like school and how much you like the holidays. If you find the changes hard, be honest with yourself about that. Your feelings are important, and they're real.

There are ways to make the transition easier, even if it initially seems complicated. Keeping some things the same, such as mealtimes, wake-up times, and even wearing similar fabrics to your school uniform, all reduce the changes you need to make when swapping modes. The fewer changes you need to make, the less anxiety you may feel. Even if you hate your school uniform, wearing a different type of shirt in the holidays now and again will mean that you won't have forgotten how it feels when it comes to wearing your school uniform at the start of term. You won't be starting all over again and needing to get used to the feel of it.

- *Busy environments*

During the school holidays, places that are usually calm will suddenly be flooded with extra people. This can be hard, especially if it's a place you use to regulate. Even areas that aren't family attractions, like supermarkets or where you walk the dog, look different, feel different, sound different and maybe even smell different.

If you need or want to go somewhere in the holidays, take time to do some extra planning. Can you buy a ticket in advance so you don't have to queue? Can you call ahead and find out when their quietest times are? Maybe even look for somewhere similar to where you usually go that isn't as well known. Planning can give you a sense of control, which lessens your anxiety. Throughout her teens, Danielle always offered to organise everything for her and her friends. Why? Because that way she had the most information and control, which kept her calm enough to go out.

Sensory-wise, wear your usual noise-cancelling headphones and consider adding some low-level noise or music you find comforting. Sunglasses and tinted glasses can help, especially if you're feeling more sensitive to the environment as your anxiety levels are on the rise.

• *Boredom*

So often, having nothing to do is the worst thing for someone's mental health. We all have times when we don't feel like doing much, and that's OK! But we need things to do to keep ourselves focused and not overwhelmed by anxiety.

A daily structure helps. Identifying a couple of times in the day when you know you are going to do a job, something creative, or even a personal care task like taking a shower will keep you active during the holidays. You may even like to draw up a timetable to remind you of what one or two things are coming up that day.

It would be easy to think that school holidays are a thing that will stop when you are an adult, but you will still have leave from your job, and if you have children yourself, then you will find that you will have parent term time and holiday modes as well. Learning to deal with the anxiety that goes with changes of mode will not only help you in the short term but also throughout life.

CHAPTER 7

Demands and Requests

We want to put this out there, plain and simple. Being a teenager is HARD!

It's a time of enormous change in how you think, and your body works. It's also a time when you want to be independent, not just in going out to places but also in what you think and believe in. All teenagers go through this, but when you're autistic/ADHD, it can seem like your teenage years are even more demanding. Why is this? Well, you might find that the thoughts and opinions you have are different to a lot of people who aren't autistic or ADHD. Perhaps you feel strongly about your views and may find it difficult to understand other people's points of view. Maybe other people also find it hard to understand your points of view! This can feel frustrating, and you may get annoyed at other people. And this is where demands and requests might cause arguments between you and others. People asking you to do things could even make you feel anxious or overwhelm you, making you uneasy.

Charlotte and Danielle struggled with people asking them to do things when they were teenagers, and sometimes they still do! There were many reasons for this, and sometimes those reasons differed for each. Let's look at why we can find being asked to do something a bit difficult sometimes.

1. *Working out what people are asking us to do*

Our first reason is how much brainpower it takes to work out what people are asking us to do! Neurotypical people can use the skills needed to work out what the request is and what they need to do, using a lot less energy than autistic/ADHD people. For us, working out what is being asked of us and how to do it can take a lot longer and leave us feeling more tired, too.

When someone asks you to do something, you have to work out their communication, make your brain work so you can work out what to do and maybe even deal with some sensory processing. All these skills can be a real challenge for us and make us feel worried and anxious.

2. *HOW someone asks you to do something*

The second reason requests can be complicated is how you receive them. Most of the time, when someone asks you to do something, they ask you in words. Both Charlotte and Danielle still struggle with this, even in adulthood. This is because even though their hearing is excellent, the way their brain understands the words is not. It takes them much longer to determine what the words mean, like when you speak a different language, and you must work out what each word means in English. Sometimes, people find understanding spoken words so tricky that they are diagnosed with something called Auditory Processing Disorder. It doesn't mean that your hearing isn't working, and it doesn't mean your brain is broken. It simply means that it takes you longer than other people to work out what the words being spoken to you mean.

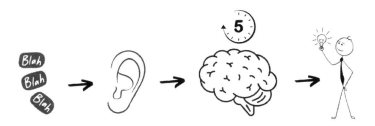

*In a brain **without** Auditory Processing Disorder, the ear receives a message, and the brain takes a few seconds or less to work it out.*

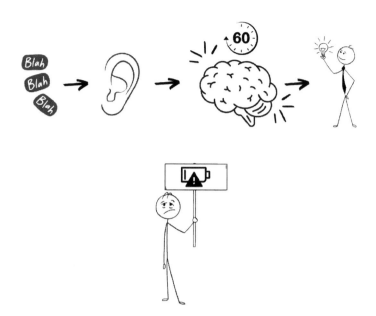

*In a brain **with** Auditory Processing Disorder, the ear receives a message fine, but the brain takes a lot longer to work out what it means. This extra work can leave a person feeling exhausted by the end of the day.*

Charlotte often describes auditory processing difficulties as being like a computer that is trying to load a programme. Suddenly, it has less memory space for other tasks, like when you try to use the internet while a computer downloads a new game. It's all slow and sluggish, and it takes far longer to do things that are usually quick. The computer gets hot, and the fan turns on. If you struggle to work out what someone has asked you to do, you have to use all your power to understand the words being said. Maybe you even get hot and wish you had a fan! Just like the computer tries to protect itself from overload, so do you and anxiety can make you feel hot and maybe stressed.

You might ask yourself if you have understood the question. Can you remember what you have to do? Will you be able to do it in an acceptable way? Before you have even managed to get your head around this, the chances are there will be another question. Someone asks you if you have understood the first question, and they expect a quick answer. We haven't even got to the request, and many factors can already make you anxious. If this sounds familiar, there are ways to make these requests easier.

If you find reading easier than listening, you can ask people to write you the request. Perhaps they can write a list for you or send you a text. If it's a regular thing you must do, pop a task reminder on your phone that repeats. This removes the parts of someone asking you to do something you find hardest. If it's a task in class, having the exercise written down can stop you from forgetting what you've been asked to do, meaning you won't feel embarrassed about forgetting, and you won't have to try and reprocess the instructions repeatedly.

If your brain doesn't have to work as hard, you can hopefully avoid a meltdown or a shutdown where it may appear to others that you are simply refusing to do as you're told, even though you know that's not the case.

3. *Fear of failure*

The third reason is something many of us with anxiety have felt before: fear of failure. It's not uncommon that people with autism or ADHD (or both) hold very high standards for themselves. We like things to be just so, and we want things to be the best they possibly can. Being "perfect" is far less stressful than getting something wrong. Getting something wrong means we must communicate about the request again and relive everything discussed in this chapter.

4. *The feeling of failing*

Then, there is the feeling of failing itself. People often try to avoid failure because facing it can be uncomfortable and challenging. Why is this?

We can feel scared of what other people think about us.

Sometimes, we avoid doing things because we're worried about what people will say if we don't do well. Maybe we don't want to be laughed at or criticised.

We feel pressure to be perfect all the time.

People around us might expect us to be perfect and successful. Failing feels like we aren't living up to these big expectations or letting down people we care about.

We think failure means we aren't good enough.

Imagine if getting a bad grade or not winning a game made you feel like you're not good enough. Many people think this way when they fail things and don't like how it feels.

We want to stay in our safe zone.

Imagine you have a cosy, safe area where everything is familiar. Stepping out into something new or challenging feels a bit scary. That's why some people avoid situations where they might fail; it is an unknown place to us, and we don't know what to do next.

Feeling upset or disappointed is a horrible feeling.

Failing can make us feel upset or disappointed. Some people don't like feeling that way, so they try to stay away from anything that might make them fail so they can avoid that feeling.

Not knowing how to handle setbacks.

We have to learn how to handle setbacks in life; we don't just know how to handle them. Some people feel nervous if they haven't learned to bounce back from challenging situations. This can be like not knowing how to get back up after falling. Until we have learned those skills, many people will avoid failure in any way they can. But if we don't fail, how will we ever know those all-important skills to pick ourselves up and carry on after falling?

Remember, everyone messes up sometimes, and it's OK! Failing is a part of learning and growing, like when you fall off a bike but figure out how to ride it better. It's not about being perfect but about trying to improve each time. Many people see failure as a challenge to improve on things. Others don't think you can fail if you try because trying anything is a success!

Rejection Sensitive Dysphoria

The last reason we will discuss here is a powerful feeling that some of us get. Usually, when you don't get the perfect score or don't follow the instructions right the first time, one of two things happens. Either the person who has given you the task assumes that you would like help to know how to do better, or the person who has given you the task decides you haven't tried hard enough.

Either way, not being perfect the first time means you must hear feedback from someone, which can be extremely hard for many people.

Some people feel an overpowering reaction when they have to hear feedback about something they have done or tried to do which hasn't been perfect. This reaction has to do with how you think other people feel about you and is far more common in those with ADHD than autism.

It's called Rejection Sensitive Dysphoria (RSD). RSD is NOT a neurodevelopmental condition like Autism and ADHD. It's a small part of being autistic/ADHD that not everyone has.

RSD is when someone feels unusually sensitive to the idea that others might not like them or could criticise them. It's like having super strong emotions, such as feeling very sad or anxious, when you think that someone might not want to be your friend or might say something mean.

Those with RSD might get these intense feelings even if the rejection or criticism isn't happening, but they think it might. It's just like anxiety when we fear what might happen, not what is happening right now. This occurs often in social situations when we worry about being judged or not fitting in.

*Rejection Sensitive Dysphoria is when you become extremely worried about people criticising you, not liking you or talking about you behind your back. It makes you feel **VERY** anxious.*

While RSD isn't an official mental health diagnosis on its own, it helps us understand how some people struggle with the fear of not being liked or accepted. It's like when you work hard on a drawing or project and want your friends or family to say they love it. If they don't react as you hope, it might make you feel sad, upset or annoyed at yourself. Even small things can make them feel sad or disappointed, and often, those with RSD are called "overly sensitive" or told they need to "toughen up a bit".

So, rejection sensitive dysphoria is when you feel very sensitive to the idea that people might not like you or the way you complete a task. This stops some of us from even trying to do anything we are asked. If we don't try, we can't be criticised for not being good enough, and we can't make people dislike us.

Sometimes, feeling this way is OK, but some might feel it more intensely. If you ever think this, talking to someone you trust, like a friend, family member, or teacher, about these feelings is OK. They can help you understand and handle them better.

Danielle suffered from severe RSD for many years. She was constantly called overly sensitive by friends, family and even teachers until her late teens. The idea of being criticised brought her such pain that she could physically feel it in her chest and stomach. Behind closed doors, there were tears about why people would view her in such a negative way, but mostly because she could see that other people her age would brush off criticism instantly, but for her, that same criticism would be hanging over her for days. The criticism consumed her thoughts, feelings, and even actions as she tried to fix it. It was excruciating, and that's the effect level we refer to when discussing RSD.

Eventually, during her late teens and early twenties, Danielle overcame RSD with the help of cognitive behavioural therapy. She still has to manage her thoughts and feelings daily. Sometimes, she feels that pain but can acknowledge it and move on. The treatment was worth it, so the wider world made her less anxious and emotional.

CHAPTER 8

Friendships

Friendship is a fundamental part of life for humans. It's all about having friends to hang out with, help when needed, and feel like you belong. But for autistic/ADHD teenagers and young people, making and keeping friends can be challenging.

In this chapter, we are going to look at the reasons why friendship causes anxiety for autistic/ADHD teenagers and young people. We will talk about many self-help ideas aimed at building confidence, making friends and finding your way through social interactions in a much easier way.

As an autistic/ADHD teenager, you can face pretty unique challenges socially. Why? Because we communicate differently to many people, we experience the world around us more intensely. We don't always get why we should behave in specific ways so we don't seem rude. These challenges can make us anxious and uncertain, particularly when making and keeping friends. Hopefully, we can give you some tips based on our personal experiences to help you find it all easier to manage.

Making and keeping friends can make us feel anxious

Trying to understand what people are feeling without them saying it or knowing when to talk and what to say can be difficult. It can make you feel unsure about yourself when you're with others, making it hard to make and keep friends. Plus, our words are constantly changing, especially for people like us. Charlotte and Danielle remember being teenagers and feeling so lost because words they thought they understood suddenly meant something different, which was very confusing.

Autistic teenagers might worry about being left out or not understood by their friends because they act or talk differently. These worries can make you feel anxious and even make it hard to talk to the friends you already have.

We've talked a lot about autistic/ADHD people being extra sensitive to things like loud noises, bright lights, or crowded places. This can be tough if your friends want to hang out in busy spots like shopping centres, cinemas, gigs or sports centres. Sometimes, these sensory things can be too much, and you might be unable to go. Then, you might feel like you're not as close to your friends. But that's not all when it comes to sensory stuff and friendships. You might feel like you must wear certain clothes or use certain things to fit in with your friends. But that's not true! You can often find items similar to the most popular trend right now but more comfortable. You can also find hacks to help you find fashions easier (see our chapter on clothing for those ideas). We get that there's pressure about this stuff and that it's not always as simple as making a few changes. This is especially true when you want to fit in and not stand out.

One piece of advice we would offer is that if you do choose to feel uncomfortable so that you blend in with the latest fashions, make sure you are kind to yourself once you get home. Remember what we said about self-care and its importance (see chapter on burnout). No one has to know how you calm your senses down or how you need a childhood toy to feel less anxious. That part is about you and what you need, not what anybody else needs.

Although friendships are complex, you can take several small steps to help. Hopefully, this will mean that you will have more positive friendship experiences. Friendship is a word that has changed its meaning over the years. Since social media came along, people have believed that friendship is down to the number of "friends" or followers you have online. Online friendships can often be much easier for neurodivergent people, and we will look at that shortly, but for now, remember that friendship is about quality, not quantity and is much more than a number.

Here are some tips:

1. *Accept yourself for who you are.*

The first step in overcoming anything is self-discovery.
It will help to be honest with yourself about who you are
and celebrate your strengths. By being open about your
strengths, challenges, and unique qualities, you can embrace
your autism/ADHD as an important part of your identity.
It's OK to acknowledge that some social situations are more
difficult than others.

This isn't going to be something that you can do overnight,
and it's also something you need to think about a fair bit.
Thinking about accepting who you are isn't something
which should be seen as a failing. It's a process of
strengthening your determination to be happy with who you
are.

2. *Work on your communication*

The second tip for overcoming your anxiety around friendship is to work on your communication and social skills. Communication and social rules are at the heart of successful friendships. These are things that your neurotypical peers may not have to do. Communication is one of the main challenges faced by autistic people, and needing to work on it is nothing to worry about or be ashamed of. Practice active listening, asking questions, and expressing yourself clearly and confidently. This can be something that you do on your own or ask a trusted person to help you with.

Charlotte and Danielle often practice communication and prepare conversations in their heads as it helps reduce anxiety. It is like being an actor and learning a script but ensuring that there is a space for improvisation. It is essential to make it clear that working on improving your social skills doesn't mean that you should force yourself to give eye contact or to work to remove any "autistic traits". It's about feeling confident that you're able to express yourself in the way you want to.

3. *Find your favourite way to communicate*

As well as working on your communication skills, look at different ways of communicating and use the various options available. Charlotte and Danielle haven't seen each other in person for two years, and they've spoken on the phone once in the last six months. But that doesn't mean they are less friends than if they were talking all the time, and that doesn't mean they don't communicate. They message each other every day. This kind of friendship reduces some of the anxiety you might feel with face-to-face friendships; for some people, they just work better.

Expectations of friendship

It can be tricky if you are eager to have friends not to have far too high expectations. This includes expectations of yourself and others. Even your closest friends need space and time, which doesn't mean your friendship is less real if you don't talk for a while.

Equally, it is important to not put too much pressure on yourself to be sociable. At times, you might need to compromise, and there might be occasions when you go to places that ordinarily you may not choose or feel comfortable with, but you do it because your friend(s) wish to do it.

Don't put too much pressure on yourself to spend too much time out of your comfort zone. If you push yourself too hard, you might risk autistic burnout, which could lead to spending time recovering away from friends.

If you are at the stage of actively seeking friends, then a good place to start is by joining clubs or groups based on your interests. You don't have to share interests with your friends, but having a common or shared interest can make finding things to chat about easier. These groups don't need to be face to face if that is too overwhelming, but make sure that you think about safety when joining online groups, especially if you ever decide to meet a person you have met online.

It is lovely to have friends and spend time with other people, but everyone, whether they have autism/ADHD or not, needs to have time on their own. This allows you to regulate, rest, and think about the friendship in a calm and measured way, which can help stop feeling overwhelmed and anxious. Remember your boundaries and that telling people about your needs is OK. It is OK to say no to invitations!

When it all seems too much

You might have read all this and still feel these suggestions are too much, but that is fine. The only person who knows what is suitable for you is YOU! If you are feeling this, you are not alone. Charlotte has been there and regularly feels like managing friendships is too much. It isn't a failure and doesn't mean you won't overcome your fears. You might tell people that you don't want friends, but you do. It just seems too terrifying and overwhelming. What it means is that you need to break down many of the steps mentioned above and take things a lot more slowly. There is no rush or race to make friends with someone. Sometimes someone you haven't known well for years will become a close friend when you realise you share the same interests.

Gradually spend time in social situations that make you feel anxious, starting with less overwhelming situations (e.g., meeting one other person for lunch) and building up to more challenging ones (e.g., going to a party with a small group of friends). Each successful experience can make you feel more confident and build your inner strength.

It would be best to have ownership over this process and always feel in control. Alongside this gradual increase in spending time with others, try to talk positively to yourself about your worth, capabilities, and potential. Replace negative beliefs about yourself with encouraging statements that help you remember your strengths and goals in life.

Whatever stage you are at, remember that:

• This is not a race to become sociable
• It is not about getting rid of your autism/ADHD

• Friendship is not about the number of friends you have!

Never stop loving your uniqueness as an autistic/ADHD individual. Always remember that your opinions, talents, and what you have to say make the world more exciting!

CHAPTER 9

Social Events

Social events can bring on a particular type of anxiety called social anxiety. Social anxiety is a specific kind of anxiety disorder. It's when someone feels highly anxious or scared about social situations where others might judge them. This fear can make them avoid social events altogether and make it hard to do everyday things like work or school. Social anxiety is focused on being anxious in social situations rather than overall anxiety, which we describe in the introduction.

Supporting yourself with social anxiety involves understanding your needs and implementing a plan to help yourself deal with these situations.

Sticking to a routine and keeping things consistent is the best way to handle your worries. A routine can help you feel calm and regulated, especially when a social event is coming up. You might be thinking, "How can I do that when the event is a change?" The key is to try to make things as normal as you can. That means fitting your social plans into your regular schedule as much as possible.

For example, if you have a family event on a Saturday afternoon, keep your Saturday morning as close to your routine as possible. Save up your brain power and that all-important executive functioning for the afternoon by spending the morning well within your comfort zone. Give yourself time to get ready, of course, so you aren't making a last-minute mad dash for it, but stick to what you would typically do as much as possible. Whether that's lying in bed and watching TV or going for a run, it doesn't matter. Don't expend all your energy before you need it!

Letting friends and family know about the difficult things you deal with at social events can be helpful. It helps them understand what you're comfortable with and where your boundaries are. When they appreciate that, it can take a bit of the pressure off when you're in social settings, which can help ease your nerves.

How to prepare for a social event

Though it may not seem like it, you can prepare for an event you feel nervous about in many ways. One of Danielle's favourite sayings, "knowledge is power", comes into its own here because the more you know before you go, the less uncertainty there is on the day. Here are a few ideas on what to look for before heading to your social event.

1. Find out as much as possible about the event

Knowing as much as possible about the social event helps you plan as much as possible. Things such as timings, dress code, and who will be there reduce the unknowns. Even if you discover that you don't know anyone else who is going, that's still information you didn't have beforehand. Sometimes, you may decide that based on the information you have found out, the event isn't suitable for you and skipping it may be the best option for your mental health. This isn't an excuse you can use all the time, though; it just shows the value of looking up the details as much as possible before attending.

Charlotte remembers going to a wedding as a teenager, and to her horror, she was seated at a table with other people her age. This was her absolute nightmare. She had assumed that she would be with her parents, not strangers with whom she had nothing in common despite the age similarity.

At the time, she was 18 and mortified by her response to the situation, which was a very public and flamboyant meltdown. Thankfully, the seating plan was altered, and she was on a table with much older people. Although she knew she would still need to communicate with them, there was much less pressure, and she was more comfortable.

If Charlotte had known this information before the wedding, the meltdown would either have happened at home or not at all. It shows how helpful it can be to know these things before a social event!

Even if the list of things you need to find out seems overwhelming...

You'll feel so much better once you get started!

Sometimes silly details like how long it takes to travel to a venue or what the scenery will look like on the way help, too. You know when you are getting close and the exact moment you will arrive. You are not nervous about getting lost or going to the wrong place. Whatever it is you feel will help you, find it out. Tell close people you're going to the event with that whatever the detail you're asking for, it would just make you feel better and more relaxed at the event itself.

2. *Learn by looking*

Lots of autistic/ADHD people learn best through visuals. Many people think of visual cues as picture cards that you use when you're children and that they're childish. This isn't true and is a big help in social settings.

Helpful visuals can be anything from photos to maps to timetables. They can guide you in different ways, like giving you directions or letting you scope out the place and people beforehand so you're not caught off guard. They're also handy for looking back on after the event, helping you feel better about how you handled things. This comes in handy when you've got to repeatedly go through similar social stuff.

Sometimes, the best visual aid is visiting a venue in person before the event so you can see what it will look like and where everything is. This isn't always possible, for example, when a wedding is in a marquee that hasn't been put up yet, but companies or venues always have photos of previous events, which you can use to give you a rough idea.

3. *Make any decisions you can before you go*

The more decisions you make before a social event that you

can, the less your brain has to work when you're out and about with friends and family. You can keep that mental energy for socialising and stop panicking when you feel pressured to decide something on the spot.

Get any clothes you might wear washed and ready before the event day so you can change your mind without any stress.

You can usually make more decisions before going out than you realise, and you can also space those decisions. You can choose an outfit ahead of an event. Danielle always chooses an outfit ahead of time and what she calls a fail-safe outfit. The fail-safe is one with minimal sensory input that she feels comfortable in. When at university, Danielle was due to go to a ball once but began to feel highly anxious in the hours before she was due to leave. After a while, she swapped from wearing her chosen dress to trousers with a top. She still looked smart, but she was so much more comfortable that her anxiety levels reduced massively. Her fail-safe outfit wasn't what she would have chosen to wear, but it was still smart enough that she could go and not look out of place. The outfit change helped calm her nerves by reducing the uncomfortable sensory feelings, but it didn't take any stress to choose it as she already had it on standby from choosing it a few days before.

Meal choices are another decision you can make easily. If you're heading out to a restaurant, check their website and make some choices before you go. You don't need to tell anyone; just let the waiter know when they come to take your order.

Practising social skills through role-playing can help tackle social anxiety. It's one time when that little voice in your head can be pretty handy. Charlotte has always done this. She rehearses conversations she might have, especially when she is heading to a restaurant. She picks out her first choice on the menu and a backup option in case the restaurant doesn't have what she wants.

Charlotte will take it a step further by practising asking for the dish, ensuring she's confident with any difficult words. When heading to a restaurant with food from a different country, words can be challenging to pronounce. You can always point to your option and show the waiter/waitress your choice.

4. *Practice some coping strategies*

Learning coping strategies to handle social anxiety, like deep breathing, positive self-talk, or mindfulness, can make a big difference. But knowing when and how to use these tricks is key. If you're not confident in how and when to use them, you will feel nervous if you try them while feeling on edge. To avoid this, ensure you've practised and felt confident about these techniques before you're in a situation where they could help you. As with most things, practice makes perfect! You can look up relaxing deep breathing exercises online.

5. *Choose someone safe to tell about your worries*

Speaking up for yourself can be challenging, but it's essential, especially in social settings. Make sure you let someone you trust know what you need and prefer. And don't forget to do this before the event even starts.

Someone to support you if needed can help you feel safe at any event.

When you build up your self-confidence and talk about what you need to feel calm and safe, you'll feel more in control and better able to handle social situations. Dealing with social anxiety is hard enough, but when you add autism or ADHD into the mix, it can be even tougher. But don't worry! There are ways you can help yourself, just as we discussed in this chapter.

In time, you will learn the best ways to do it. Being sociable can be tricky sometimes, but it can also be amazing! You might need some time to recover and rest afterwards, but by putting things in place before you go to a social event, you can have a great time!

CHAPTER 10

Burnout

Burnout means feeling completely worn out because of too much stress, especially from work or caring for others. It can make you feel tired, detached, and like you can't do things well anymore. For people who are autistic/ADHD, burnout is often used to describe feelings of exhaustion due to trying to live in a world that isn't always built with us in mind. The reasons for burnout in autistic people can differ slightly from those with ADHD, but these reasons often overlap due to how similar autism and ADHD can be and how many people are diagnosed with both.

Autistic burnout is when someone who is autistic feels worn out, both mentally and emotionally. It happens when they've been dealing with a lot of stress or things that bother them for a long time. During this time, they might find it hard to concentrate, feel more sensitive to things like noise or light, and may want to spend more time alone. They also lose skills and feel chronic exhaustion. These feelings continue for three months or more[1].

ADHD burnout feels and looks similar to autistic burnout. It can result from prolonged periods of trying to keep up with daily responsibilities without the proper support or coping strategies. It can also happen when individuals push themselves too hard without taking breaks or practising self-

1   *Defining Autistic Burnout. Dora M Raymaker et al. Autism Adulthood. 2020.*

care. Again, it involves loss of skills and chronic exhaustion and must continue for three months or more.

One significant thing to note is that you cannot receive a formal diagnosis of burnout. It is a feeling and a result of struggling with your formal diagnosis of autism and/or ADHD.

Autistic/ADHD burnout and anxiety often cross over and get so tangled up that you can't tell which one is causing certain feelings. Both burnout and stress can make you feel tired, sad, confused and nervous. They can also make each other worse, so it can be tricky to work out whether you are anxious or burnt out.

Lots of things can contribute to burnout.

Burnout and anxiety are often caused by the same things, too. Sensory overload, lots of socialising and changes in routine can make you feel anxious, and when you have been feeling them for a long time, they can cause burnout. When we feel anxious for a long time, it can make autistic burnout worse. Anxiety is having constant worry, and it can tire us out and make it hard to handle things. When we're already in burnout, feeling overwhelmed, the anxiety can get even stronger. That's because we start noticing things we can't do as easily as we used to, which can make us feel even more stressed.

Burnout can be a survival instinct in some ways. Thinking of it as a way to bounce back can be helpful. It's your body saying that you need time to recover. When you're going through autistic/ADHD burnout, it's important to know the signs and do things to take care of yourself. That means finding ways to deal with stress, looking after yourself, and asking for help when needed. Here are some things you can try:

1. *Learn to recognise the signs of burnout*

If you understand and recognise the signs of burnout, you can take steps to try and stop it in its tracks. Symptoms and signs can include feeling a lot more tired, being more sensitive to things like light, sound and smell and feeling sad and emotional all the time. Don't ignore it if you feel that way; that won't help you feel better. Use the following few points to try and help yourself better.

2. *Put self-care first*

When you think you might be in burnout, you should make looking after yourself the most important thing you do. Self-care is anything that helps you relax, recharge your energy levels, and reduce any feelings of stress. Self-care activities can be anything that helps, but they usually include things like meditation, deep breathing, spending time outdoors in the fresh air, or enjoying your favourite hobbies. Self-care is about recognising that you don't feel great and doing things that help you recover and feel better.

3. Set boundaries

Setting boundaries means you decide how much of something is too much, and you don't let yourself go over the amount you set yourself. It's about prioritising what you need the most that's going to help you recover. So, for example, if talking on the phone drains your energy levels, perhaps you set the boundary that you will only speak on the phone twice a week. The rest of the time, messaging will have to do, even if your friends ask to talk on the phone.

That boundary means you are making daily life a little bit easier for yourself and giving yourself a chance to recover.

It's OK to say no to extra commitments or responsibilities when overwhelmed. You must tell others about the boundaries you put in place so they know you're trying to help yourself get better.

4. *Keep an eye on sensory triggers*

When you're overwhelmed and maybe stressed, you might notice your senses becoming more sensitive! A smell or sound that might not have bothered you too much before could now be unbearable. For Danielle, an increased sense of smell, which can make her physically jump or shout when she smells something unpleasant, is a sure sign she needs to be wary of burnout. Be kind to your senses. This might involve creating a sensory-friendly environment, using noise-cancelling headphones, wearing comfortable clothing, or taking breaks in quiet spaces when needed.

5. *Try and keep to your daily routine.*

When you are in burnout, it can be useful to keep to your When you are experiencing burnout, it can be helpful to keep to your daily routine as much as possible. This can reduce anxiety and make you feel stable during periods of burnout. Remember that being out of routine can cause anxiety, which in turn can increase the possibility of burnout.

6. *Reach out for help*

Don't be scared to reach out to trusted friends, family members, and those who understand your experiences. They could offer empathy, validation, and encouragement. Connecting with others who share similar experiences can help reduce feelings of isolation, which will be incredibly helpful, especially when experiencing burnout.

Remember that managing autistic/ADHD burnout is an ongoing process, and it's essential to be patient with yourself as you find your way through your unique challenges and strengths. Everybody will have a different experience of burnout, and at the time, it can appear that there is no way out, but there is. Be kind to yourself and listen to your body!

CHAPTER 11

Safe Spaces

When people think of a safe space, they tend to think of these beautiful sensory rooms, all kitted out with the latest equipment. Bubble tubes and fairy lights, with giant cushions on the floor for you to sink into. As lovely as that would sound for some of us, that isn't what a safe space is. A safe space can be anything you want, depending on your needs and what you find the most calming.

Of course, we have the more typical ones such as sensory rooms, a quiet room at school or maybe a den in your bedroom. These can work exceptionally well, but they may not be necessary or what you need. So, what is a safe space? And what do we use them for?

When we talk about a safe space for autistic people, what we mean is somewhere where a person can feel physically and emotionally secure. A safe space gives an autistic/ADHD person a place to let out their feelings and emotions, lower their anxiety levels and regulate their feelings so they become calmer. How each autistic/ADHD person does this is entirely individual, so each safe space will usually have a unique set-up.

It's essential to recognise that what triggers the need for a safe space is also different in each of us. Maybe it's the need to stim very loudly. Stimming, or self-stimulation, is when

113

we make repetitive movements to either stimulate or calm the feelings in our bodies. For example, some of us bounce our knees up and down when we feel like we have too much energy, or maybe we make noises such as humming when we feel nervous. Stimming can disturb others, but we still need to do it, so some people use their safe space to express their stims without being judged by others.

Another possible use is if someone struggles to control emotional outbursts. They need to have that outburst, or else they could end up in a meltdown, so they use a safe space to feel angry, sad or extremely happy away from other people. In this chapter, we will discuss how to design and use a safe space when you feel anxious. From the usual to unusual, the only thing that matters is that your safe space reduces your anxiety so that you can rejoin your lesson or household once you feel better.

Charlotte's son has a very unusual safe space. He and his Dad have an old Renault Five, with which they go on adventures and do some basic maintenance tasks. Charlotte's son will sometimes sit in the car in the garage to regulate as he finds the smell and feel of the vehicle very calming. This might not be the most typical safe space, but how it reduces his anxiety and helps him to regulate can't be argued. It works.

You may have been guided or told about your safe space as a child. Many parents must work out what their child needs from a safe space at a very young age when their child can't communicate. It's not uncommon that these spaces don't change for a long time, and often, they stop helping the child. As you grow older and start heading towards adulthood, you can begin to think about where and what your safe space will look like. To do that, here are some tips and ideas on what to think about when creating your very own safe space!

Charlotte's son sits in their car in the garage when he needs a safe space because he finds it comforting.

How to design your own safe space

The first thing to remember when designing your safe space is:

You must be able to regulate (control your feelings and actions) and be at peace with your thoughts.

You need to feel safe and secure in it.

The second thing you must be aware of is your sensory profile. We don't mean that you need some vast assessment from a professional on your sensory likes and dislikes. It is simply an awareness of whether you feel calmer when a room is light or dark. Do you feel more relaxed with noise or silence? Do moving objects help you regulate, or do you need everything to be still? This information will help you design a room or space just for you. It doesn't matter what anyone else wants; this is only about you.

In this example, we will assume that your safe space is a room. As we have already said, it could be anywhere! Danielle sometimes uses an inflatable hot tub as her safe space. At other times, she has a room in the house. Both are designed with huge amounts of fairy lights. Both have walls and curtains to keep her hidden from others, and if needed, Danielle listens to the natural sounds of waves crashing or rivers running on her headphones. Where possible, darkness is hugely helpful to Danielle in helping her regulate. So, wherever you choose or use (including a room in school), think about the following:

1. *Colour schemes*

Consider using calming, neutral colours on the walls and in the decor.

Avoid overly bright or contrasting colours that may be overwhelming.

If you find bright colours calming, or they help you distract yourself from your anxiety, choose posters or photos that provide a visual stimulus (when you gain comfort from staring at an object for a long time).

If you can't change the colours of the walls or decor, but the colour is an important source of calm for you, ask to leave a book in your safe space that displays those colours. Maybe even a DVD of a wildlife show with vivid colours of bright environments and a portable DVD player.

2. *Declutter*

Keep the room organised and clutter-free as much as possible. This will reduce visual and sensory distractions and can often feel less stressful.

Tidying and taking items out of a room is up to you. Maybe you feel like you want to hide amongst objects, or many items around you overwhelm you.

If the safe space room at school is a shared space, ask for a room divider if you need lots of objects or none at all, so there is a space within the room you can use.

3. *Furniture*

Move furniture to create a clear path to where you would like to sit, stand or lie down.

Move any obstacles from your path, as you may not be paying attention if you're on the edge of a meltdown. Falling over could trigger a full-blown meltdown, which you actively try to avoid.

Get rid of furniture with sharp edges and choose furniture with rounded edges to prevent injuries.

Use soft and comfortable furnishings, such as plush pillows, blankets, and rugs, to provide sensory comfort.

Use comfortable and supportive furniture, such as ergonomic chairs or sensory-friendly seating options.

Think about adjustable furniture or furniture that can be easily changed to meet your evolving sensory needs. For example, chairs that recline so you can go from sitting to lying down if necessary. Some chairs vibrate for those with back injuries, and these can give fantastic proprioceptive feedback.

If your safe space in school only has chairs, and you would like to lie down, see if your school could find a spare bed or some large cushions which would be placed on the floor.

4. *Lighting*

Look at blackout blinds if you need the room to be completely dark.

Dark rooms can help projection lamps (e.g. those that project stars onto the ceiling) seem more vivid.

Fairy lights can be static, or they can flash in patterns. If colour is a huge comfort, check out the different colour light bulbs you can get, or try fibre optic lamps.

Natural daylight can make us feel much better, and nice views of grass, trees and nature can be incredible.

If you use a shared room at school, consider sleep masks or sunglasses to dull light if the curtains are open. If you need a blackout blind or fairy lights, talk to staff about how you can make that happen.

5. *Sound*

Soundproofing a room properly is very expensive, but there are ways you can make a room quieter.

Consider the furniture layout, e.g. if your room is near a busy road, then it might be better to move the bed away from the window.

Soft furnishings like blankets, cushions, and rugs can absorb echoey sounds, which some people can find stressful.

If you use a shared safe space, noise-cancelling earplugs or headphones are very helpful!

6. *Textures and materials*

Choose materials for furniture and decor that are comfortable to touch and don't have a strong smell.
If you find these helpful, include sensory-friendly materials like soft textiles, weighted blankets, or fidget-friendly items.

7. *Personalise*

Make your space a reflection of who you are, and don't be afraid to make it your own.

Adding your touches and personal items can help to create a sense of comfort and ownership.

If it helps, take an item to school with you that you find comforting and use it in a safe space.

8. *Shopping tips*

If you want to include sensory items, it can be cheaper if you remove words such as "autism" from any online searches. For example, search for "weighted blanket" rather than "weighted blanket for autism", as this can increase the cost.

CHAPTER 12

Sleep and Anxiety

Finding it hard to sleep, or worrying about sleep in general, is something many people go through at some stage. Don't ever think you are alone if you're struggling with sleep; it is much more common than you think!

When it comes to anxiety affecting our sleep, it usually comes down to one of two problems.

1. When you feel anxious or worried about falling asleep. For example, it takes ages to fall asleep, and you worry you'll be too tired to get through the next day.

2. Something entirely unrelated to sleep is making you feel anxious. For example, your mind is bustling and won't be quiet. You can't relax because you're thinking about other things.

You can do many things to help yourself break free from either of these problems, but you might not get the result you want immediately. These things need to be worked on. Whether difficulties with sleeping are new to you or something you've experienced all your life, there are ways you can help yourself and start doing it straight away. Here are a few ideas and tips for you.

1. Create a bedtime structure

Create a calming and consistent bedtime structure that includes reading a book, taking a warm bath, or listening to calming music. Consistency is the key here. If you do the same things over and over again before bedtime, it helps signal to the brain that it's time to wind down and prepare for sleep.

Being consistent doesn't mean being so rigid with your structure or routine that you miss out on evenings, for example. Having some flexibility within the structure is a good thing. If you stick to an evening structure down to the second, it can cause anxiety.

Danielle's son is ten years old and has a structure for his bedtime every night. While he does the same things, many of them can happen in any order, and it doesn't matter if they happen a little later than usual. He is rigid about the time he starts to watch his evening film. He watches the same film every night before bed and presses play at EXACTLY 7 pm. If, for any reason, he has to press pause, he will skip the film to where it should be, assuming he has been watching it without any interruptions since 7 pm.

Being rigid with the film timings can sometimes make him very anxious. Danielle has tried encouraging him to press play a minute or two early, but he hasn't agreed. This is because the film represents her son's countdown to lights out. He uses the film each night to judge how much time he has left to use his electronics and he knows roughly at what part of the film he will receive his evening medication.

Despite the film timing being non-negotiable for him, most other tasks within his evening structure are. He has become very flexible regarding timings and order of things like brushing his teeth, using the toilet and putting his toys away.

These tasks, plus a few others, can happen at any point in the last hour of the film and changing the order does not cause him any stress or anxiety. After the film, Danielle's son has time to relax with certain toys in his bed until he falls asleep.

So, whilst a structure signals to your brain that sleep is on the way, keep it flexible where you can so that you're not increasing your anxiety levels right before bed.

2. *Create a bedroom environment which is right for you*

This is a stumbling block that we see time and time again. If you ask someone what a sensible sleeping environment looks like, they will most likely say things like a dark room with no noise, etc. For many people (especially neurotypical people), this is true! A silent, dark environment will bring a solid night's sleep. But this is not true for everyone.

When you have an autistic or ADHD brain, you experience the world around you very differently. This is especially true when it comes to your senses. Having the correct sensory input while asleep is just as important as having it during the day. Without the correct sensory input, you will likely feel as anxious as when battling different sight, smell and sound levels during daylight hours. So, this tip is about discovering what sensory input is correct for you to sleep with.

Charlotte sleeps best when cool, with some lights on and always with the radio playing quietly. Her son sleeps best with a bright light and two or three sounds playing. Neither Danielle nor her son can sleep without a fan, even if it's below-freezing temperatures outside.

If you need light and sound so that you can sleep, that's ok!

It can be hard sometimes to explain to people why you need such a different sleeping environment than anyone else in your house. If sleeping in a dark and quiet room isn't working for you, talk to your family or carers about ideas you want to try. Any calming sounds or music, or perhaps low-level or bright lighting. Try a few things out and see how you feel the next day. You may need a few goes before you determine what you truly need.

Bedding is something to think about, too. However hot it is in the summer, Charlotte has to have a cover. She also finds it helpful to have a weighted blanket which offers her consistent deep pressure throughout the night. These are also available from some suppliers in a cooling version for the summer.

Pyjamas are also hugely important to getting your nighttime

sensory input right. It took Charlotte almost 40 years to find the pyjamas that she found comfortable. Perhaps you need one style of pyjamas for the winter and another for the summer.

Having the right environment for YOU to sleep in is the best way to satisfy your brain's sensory needs and create a safe environment.

3. *Before your bedtime*

Your sleep doesn't just rely on the area/room you sleep in; it is also affected by what you have done during the day. We have talked about the importance of doing things in other chapters and not refusing to do activities because the idea of these activities makes you anxious. One reason for this is because you need to be tired to sleep. This might seem obvious, but at times of heightened anxiety or low mood, you can feel exhausted when you have not done anything at all.

Think of it as your brain needing to be fed certain things to function in a balanced way. To keep your body healthy, you need a mixture of vegetables and protein and a balanced diet. To keep our brains healthy, we need the right mix of physical activity, mental activity, and physical and mental rest. This can be a tricky balance to find, but you may find that it is harder to sleep on days when you have either done nothing or done too much physical or mental activity.

For this reason, a great idea is to think about how your day went during the early evening. If maybe you believe you haven't used your brain enough or you haven't used your body enough, you can use those couple of hours before getting ready for bed to balance things out. Has today been a maybe a bit too physically restful? We all need pyjama days, but going for a quick walk or doing some yoga can help your body use up those extra bits of energy. Perhaps you haven't used your brain enough and binge-watched a series on TV. Maybe do a few puzzles or read up on some facts you didn't know before. It's all about feeling balanced before bedtime.

4. *Events of the day and events of tomorrow*

Along with early mornings, bedtime is a typical time to start feeling anxious. When your brain doesn't have much to focus on, those anxious thoughts can rise to the surface far more quickly.

An excellent way to deal with this is by talking to someone you trust or writing in a journal. Imagine that as you speak or write, or maybe even record yourself talking into your phone or laptop, your head is slowly emptying of all those racing thoughts of anxiety. This leaves your head feeling free and clear during the night, reducing the risk of those thoughts getting in the way of a good night's sleep.

Danielle frequently writes things down before she goes to sleep or even when she wakes up in the middle of the night. Sometimes, it's a task she needs to add to her to-do list, and the anxiety of forgetting about it in the morning keeps her awake. Sometimes, it's just an anxious thought. She tells herself she will look into it, writes down the anxious thought and feels like a weight has been lifted because she has put that thought "on hold".

By journalling or talking things through, you are acknowledging your anxious thoughts. This can help free up valuable space in your brain, allowing it to turn off and help you get a much better night's sleep.

5. *Screen time*

You will probably be told by parents or carers to "turn off your tablet/computer/game and limit screen time" in the hours before bed. This isn't them being boring; this is because there is a mountain of research that says the light given off by screens can limit your ability to sleep.

This isn't the case for everyone, but it can be a good idea to start by reducing how much you use screens in the hour before bed. Look for a more soothing pre-bedtime routine like reading a book, puzzle, or craft activity.

If you are using your phone before bed, stay off social media. Social media sites are full of statements and photos that can send your anxiety sky-high. We know it's easier said than done, but any website that might make you feel insecure or upset should be avoided as much as possible before you settle down for the night.

Don't sit & scroll through social media right up until bedtime

6. *Reset if you need to*

Sometimes, even if we do all the right things, we still can't sleep. Lying in bed wide awake is not usually helpful if you want to sleep. If this happens, you can reset your bedtime routine/structure and start again.

You can re-do the whole thing or just part of it. It might mean washing your face again, changing your pyjamas, or anything you usually do to signal your brain that it's time for sleep. If you have a hot drink while in bed, grab another one and read a few more pages. This can be helpful if you have engaged in a conversation before bed that's woken your brain up too much, or maybe you've had an idea that's excited you!

Danielle has to reset frequently for both her and her son. For Danielle, the reason is usually an overactive brain which has come up with an idea right before bedtime.

Danielle doesn't re-do her entire evening structure. After writing down the thoughts in her head, she picks a few parts that distract her brain away from the idea enough that she can calm her thoughts and go to sleep.

For her son, the sensory parts of his bedtime structure are usually used to reset him. The light goes on for a while, and his fan goes off. He may have an ice lolly, which is particularly calming for him. Then it's lights off and fan on as it would be, and a mini reset has regulated him enough to sleep.

7. *Relaxing exercises*

Exploring different relaxing exercises, like deep breathing, relaxing your muscles slowly, or imagining calming scenes, can be helpful. This can lower stress and make it easier to relax before bed. Remember, what works for one person might not work for everyone. So, keep an open mind, try different methods, and see what helps you. Also, it's important to give these methods some time to work. Trying them just once may not show their proper effect, which can be challenging, but it's worth the effort.

Some can try all of the above but can still not sleep. This can create a cycle of frustration, anger, and, yes, you have guessed it - anxiety!

If you reach this point and have tried everything people have suggested, it might be worth chatting with your GP to see if they have any advice. Make sure they know you are autistic or ADHD because, as you know by now, our brains often need different things compared to others.

Waking in the middle of the night

All the ideas we've discussed are significant when considering how to go to sleep. What people seem to easily forget is to evaluate the quality of sleep and how long you sleep.

If you're suffering from anxiety or depression, waking up in the night can be a problem as you start to worry about things. When Charlotte was first diagnosed with depression as a teenager, she would often wake up around 2 am and worry.

When the house is quiet and still, it can be easy for your thoughts to run away with themselves. With very few distractions at that time, you may find yourself overthinking and focused on your anxious thoughts. You might feel lonely as others are asleep. Feeling lonely can make negative feelings and emotions seem a lot bigger than they are, meaning breaking out of those negative thoughts can be a lot trickier.

Anxiety has a way of messing with your body's sleep cycle, so it's not surprising that people with anxiety find themselves waking up in the middle of the night quite often. It makes us feel groggy in the morning, too.
Of course, not everyone will find they wake up in the middle of the night, but if you do, here are some ideas to help you get back to sleep.

1. *Start with the basics*

Work out if you need the toilet or a drink of water. This might sound silly or obvious, but our autistic/ADHD brains don't always tell us straight away if we need those things. If you're trying to get back to sleep, do both. If you need either, it can help a lot with drifting back off.

2. *Change your environment*

Try heading into a different room for a quick change of scene. Keep the lights low if you need darkness to sleep, as you don't want to wake your brain up too much! Stay off screens if you can, and don't read anything which takes too much effort. It's about your body and brain recognising when you head back to bed that it's time to sleep.

3. *Occupy your brain... a bit...*

Occupying your brain without waking up too much can be a complex balancing act. What you're trying to do is stop yourself from concentrating on negative or anxious thoughts whilst not waking yourself up.

Listening to music or a podcast can help. You can find a series of podcasts on the BBC website called "Boring

Talks". Topics range from car boots to farting and are, as the title suggests, boring! But they keep your brain occupied without sparking any interest that wakes you up!

4. *Journalling*

Back to our good old friend, the journal. Maybe you need to do some low-level processing or empty your brain of thoughts so you can get back off to sleep.

Don't be fooled!

The biggest mistake we see people make is believing they don't need to sleep because they're not tired. While we all need different amounts of sleep, more often, we don't sleep because we are unable to relax, not because we simply are not tired enough to sleep.

Remember, the number of hours you sleep is more important than a "sensible" bedtime. If you sleep fewer hours by going to bed at 9pm than if you go to bed at 11pm, then 11pm would be the best option. You don't want a 3am bedtime, of course, but aim for the number of hours that will give you good quality sleep.

CHAPTER 13

Food and Anxiety

Fussy eaters

Charlotte is a self-proclaimed "fussy eater" and doesn't like the term. She sees little point in being made to eat something that you don't like. If you had a pet that didn't want a particular food, you wouldn't keep buying them that food and expect them to eat it.

Charlotte has found throughout her life that there is often an unseen social pressure to eat what others are eating. This pressure can come from family, friends, or even what we think people expect to be "normal". For example, in the UK, traditionally, turkey is eaten at Christmas. If you don't like turkey, then this could cause anxiety, especially if there was a chance that you were going to be put in a situation of being served turkey at Christmas. It is easy to feel that you are judged by others, particularly with comments like, "Doesn't everybody like that?" or, "Try it, you might like it!" These viewpoints of others are a massive cause of anxiety when having to eat, especially if it is out of your typical environment or family unit.

Whilst day to day, you may not feel that having a limited diet is a cause of anxiety to you, if you are going to eat at someone else's house or a restaurant, you may feel that this becomes more of an issue. For example, you may not be able to eat anything you are served at someone's house, or there might not be anything on the menu you feel you can eat. If Charlotte eats at a restaurant, she finds that she likes some aspects of meals. This in itself is a massive cause of anxiety because she has to communicate more than if she wanted the whole meal that was on the menu. Once she overcomes that hurdle, she has the anxious wait to see if what they bring her is what she asked for.

Other people might think you don't care about your health and nutrition if you are a fussy eater. This is not the case, and for most autistic people, food choices have little or nothing to do with what is good for you. It tends to be more about what you CAN eat than what you CHOOSE. This doesn't mean, though, that you don't value your health, and it doesn't mean that you are not concerned about what nutrients your body is getting. It can be difficult if people comment, "You need to eat your five a day!" as this not only reiterates your feelings but also raises concerns about what others might think about you.

Lastly, having a limited or restricted diet is the fear of trying new food. You might be desperate to try new foods, but the anxiety surrounding this is too big. You may have a heightened sense of particular tastes, textures or smells, which means the fear of trying new foods is overwhelming. This, in turn, can also make you feel that you are not having control of your own body, which again can be a cause of different anxiety stemming from not being able to try new foods. So, if trying new foods is difficult, how can you do it without causing a lot of anxiety? Here's some tips:

1. *Start slowly*

Introduce new foods gradually, starting with small portions or adding new items to familiar dishes. If you find it hard to eat food that's a particular colour or texture, don't try to eat an entire portion, just tasting it can be enough.

2. *Choose a safe space*

Choose a safe environment to try new foods. You might be able to try food at home, either with a trusted adult or on your own, far easier than it is in a more public environment.

3. *Have options*

Make sure you have options, so you have something else to eat if you cannot eat or try the new food. Don't go hungry because today wasn't the right day to try a new food!

4. *Prepare the food yourself.*

Preparing the food can help you feel in control and give you ownership over your eating. Cooking and preparing an unknown food can often make it easier to try.

5. *Experiment!*

Experimenting with different cooking methods, textures, and presentations to make new foods more appealing helps you learn what you do and don't like. For example, if you don't like raw carrots, try roasting or steaming them instead. Charlotte also finds that shape matters. She enjoys eating carrot batons, but she doesn't like sliced carrots.

The way you eat

This is a topic that isn't often talked about when you read about challenges surrounding food and autism/ADHD. However, it is very real.

Charlotte knows she eats in a way which appears unusual to many. Like a lot of autistic people, she prefers to take apart her food. This is so that she is able to process eating the different sections of foods like pizza one at a time or in an order of my choice. Charlotte eats sandwiches starting with the crust. This gives her senses the chance to get used to the smell of the filling before she has to taste it.

Charlotte has also been told by people that she doesn't use cutlery properly. Like most people with dyspraxia she found learning how to master using cutlery a challenge and as an adult this is still a challenge and can be painful. She is always aware that people might make a comment because of the unusual way she uses cutlery, and this is an added anxiety Charlotte experiences when eating.

Spilling food and drink also happens regularly and although Charlotte is always thinking of ways not to spill things, it doesn't mean that it happens any less. When it does happen she is always aware of the anxiety the embarrasment causes as well as how she will clear it up if it does happen.

The good news is that most people are understanding of the additional challenges that we experience in these areas, and are happy to be helpful in any way they can.

Quantity

Many autistic/ADHD people experience times when they may under or over eat. If you feel that food is controlling your life to the extent that it's taking over, make sure you get help. Some challenges around your relationship with food could be linked directly to your autism/ADHD but having autism/ADHD doesn't mean that you can't have a "stand alone" eating disorder as well. If you feel that you are suffering from a potential eating disorder it is essential that you get that help and we would advise you not to read the remainder of this section as it may conflict with the support that you would need for a specific eating disorder.

Comfort eating

The term comfort eating is used quite a lot. It is when we eat more food than we should do because we think it makes us feel better. Comfort eating might serve as a coping mechanism to deal with the stress or anxiety of social situations and/or sensory overload. The repetitive and predictable nature of eating, especially particular food or food types, can provide comfort and a sense of control and predictability in an otherwise unpredictable world.

You might also find that the comfort comes from a sensory perspective and that certain textures or flavours of food may be particularly soothing for you, which might mean you seek out these foods at times when you are feeling overwhelmed or distressed, regardless of the time of day and whether you are hungry or not.

If you have ADHD, especially if you're impulsive, you may find that the reasons for comfort eating are similar but you have more challenges around impulsivity control. This means that the episodes happen more often or you eat bigger quantities when they do happen.

When it comes to anxiety, whilst the initial feeling following eating makes you feel calmer and increases a chemical called dopamine in the brain, shortly afterwards this can and does change to a feeling of regret and guilt which actually makes anxiety worse.

Autistic/ADHD people also experience the opposite to comfort eating. For some, the difficulty will be around working out if you need food and water or not. Without understanding these signs, you can easily end up missing meals which quickly becomes part of your routine and eventually becomes a more serious problem. If you don't get enough food and drink then you are more likely to feel anxious or have less ability to overcome it.

Whether you feel that you are more likely to eat too much food too often or not enough food not often enough, the self help that you can do for either is similar. Although there is no one-size-fits-all approach, here are a few strategies that might help you.

1. *Routine*

Having regular meal and snack times can help lower the chances of you eating without thinking about it or not wanting to eat. In time you are likely to find the routine creates predictability which gives you comfort and means you are more likely to eat the right amount of food at the right time.

2. *An all-round approach*

Looking at approaches such as mindfulness means you can focus on the sensory experience of eating. This will make eating more comfortable and enjoyable as well as making you more aware of your hunger and fullness cues.

3. *Healthy foods*

Find foods that are healthy and tasty which will in turn reduce your desire to binge on less healthy options. Or, if you are finding it hard to eat regularly, it will make you more likely to feel positive about food.

As we said at the start of this section, if you are having

significant challenges around your relationship with food, don't delay in getting professional support.

CHAPTER 14

The Overactive Brain

Something that autism, ADHD and anxiety all have in common is their speed of thought or thinking. Whether we are hyperactive, making connections between patterns or worrying and feeling anxious, we often feel like our thoughts are racing through our heads at tremendous speed. These racing thoughts are usually described as the brain being overactive. The thoughts are coming so fast that you can't even write them down quick enough to keep up before the next one enters your head. A lot of the time, these racing thoughts cause us to feel anxious.

Charlotte remembers being told regularly to use her brain as a teenager. She wanted to scream, "My brain doesn't stop!" and it is still the same today. It is an incredible gift to have a neurodivergent brain, but the brain has a lot to answer when it comes to anxiety. Having an overactive brain is one of those things that might appear alien if you have never experienced it, but if you are like us, then you will definitely get it.

The overactive brain vs the logical brain

Charlotte's brain is unable to carry out one task. We don't mean several activities at once; we mean the anxiety triggering her overactive brain. She starts doing a task, and her brain instantly thinks about all the possible issues with that particular task.

This kind of overactivity is usually triggered by another person's comment or a glance. When Charlotte was 12, she was in a choir. They were in a competition. They came second in the competition, but the adjudicator commented that it was a shame that one of the singers was not looking at the conductor and was fiddling with their earrings. Charlotte knew who it was, but her brain decided that she was the culprit. She felt she had let everyone down. Charlotte spent ages blaming herself.

Eventually, another member of the choir pointed out to her that it couldn't possibly have been her as she didn't have her ears pierced and didn't wear earrings. This might appear incredibly obvious, but her brain had gone into overdrive and wouldn't stop. Even after she had been reassured, it took a few days for her brain to stop going over this fully.

Another area of overactivity both Charlotte and Danielle's brain's are good at is catastrophising. We don't mean exaggerating something that has happened to make it sound worse. We mean thinking about every possible catastrophe before the event. If you plan to go on a quick dog walk, you might go through all the things that could go wrong first. What if you fall over? The dog might get injured. You might lose the dog or get lost if you decide to go on a new route. These are just some of the ideas our brains would eagerly process. By the time it has finished, the prospect of a relaxing walk has turned into a potentially life-ending activity. With a brain like this, it isn't surprising that it can get anxious.

It's often impossible to stop our brains from going into these overactive spirals. But we can learn to reassure ourselves. The trick is to allow your brain to have its moment of doom and gloom, then switch that negative thought around. It takes practice, but it really does work!

A simple exercise that you can start is to answer the worry of your overactive brain (OB) with a thought from your logical brain (LB). Gradually, you will be able to reverse what would have been an anxiety-provoking thought into a reassurance. Let's take the dog-walking scenario as an example.

Your overactive brain brings up all sorts of worries and potential problems. Let's see how you could answer those problems with a logical thought.

OB: "What if you fall over?"

LB: "You have fallen over before but have always been ok."

OB: "What if you lose your dog?"

LB: "Your dog doesn't leave your side, so it is very unlikely this will happen."

OB: "What if you get lost going on a new route."

LB: "Whilst you don't have the best sense of direction, your smartphone has maps, so you can find your way back easily."

It is important in this that you don't dismiss the concerns of your overactive brain but rather rationalise them. This is similar to telling someone you have a concern. If they dismiss the concern, then you are left feeling uneasy, unsure, and possibly more anxious, but for a different reason.

Your overactive brain might say, "I am worried about going out with my friends at the weekend because I don't have anything to wear."

Someone might dismiss your worry by saying, "You have loads of clothes; don't be silly."

What you and others should say to help your overactive brain is, " I am sure you have something, as you have lots of clothes, but it can be hard to work out what to wear for social events. Would you like help choosing?"

Remember to ask your logical brain what it thinks. It can help calm down your overactive brain.

When an overactive brain is labelled as "silly"

When someone, or yourself, makes out your thought is silly, it causes more anxiety. Not only are you being told/thinking that you are wrong, but someone else/you are ignoring your challenges. When someone supports you/you support yourself, your concerns are justified, and you are reassured and given help.

Remember, it's not just other people who shouldn't dismiss your anxiety and make it out to be silly. This is a job for you, too. Yes, you are worried. Is the worry something that is likely to happen? Probably not, but that doesn't matter. Be kind to yourself, acknowledge that you're finding this particular thing difficult, and then plan for a way to support yourself that makes you feel less anxious.

Working out how to reduce the anxiety of an overactive brain

Danielle also has a very overactive brain. Counsellors often tell her that she has a very creative brain that comes up with all sorts of scenarios professionals couldn't think of if they tried. Like Charlotte, Danielle thinks through all the possible scenarios her brain creates before an event or typical day. But for her, the anxiety is shown through the number of things she feels she needs to pack "just in case" there is a worldwide disaster in the 5-minute walk between her house and the village shop.

Over the years, Danielle has earned the nickname "practical Danielle" because no matter what happens or what is needed on any type of trip, Danielle has it. For Danielle, though, this makes packing for ANY reason unbelievably stressful.

Just like Charlotte, Danielle plays through every eventuality in her head and works out what she might need to survive them. She packs everything from make-up, first aid kits, chargers, and vast amounts of clothing. Packing is exhausting and massively anxiety-provoking, sometimes leading to so much panic that she has to stop and regulate so that she can ground herself and start again. What Danielle realised was that there was a way to manage this anxiety, even if it led to other people making comments. She packs what she needs for each one of her worries.

She is always the one with the most enormous bag compared to anyone else because it's the best way to keep her anxiety at bay. Danielle doesn't worry about all those scenarios she played out in her head anymore because she knows she is ready for any of them.

Of course, there are downsides to carrying huge bags of belongings around, not to mention the back and shoulder aches. People ask why she has so much stuff for a trip to the park, etc. But for Danielle, it means that her anxiety is reduced and space is freed up in her brain so she can enjoy her trip out, whether it's 5 minutes or 5 days. She laughs with others if they make the odd joke and doesn't mind being the one with the identity of carrying "a Mary Poppins bag" that seems to be bottomless. The main thing is that this method works for her.

Danielle packs whatever she needs to calm her anxieties.

When our worries come true

None of us can see into the future, so there will be times when your overactive brain predicts something that then does come true. This has happened to Charlotte and Danielle several times, and both have actually found it relatively helpful. It has helped them feel justified in rehearsing the negative event, which makes us more resilient in the long run.

You may feel panicked if your anxieties actually happen. It might even make you think you must prepare for even more eventualities. A way to stop your anxiety spiralling is to keep a note of how many times your worries actually do come true. That way, you can see that the more significant worries aren't happening regularly.

Suppose you feel your brain is so overactive that you can't possibly prepare for all these different eventualities it's coming up with. In that case, it can be helpful to work out how you deal with the worst that could happen. Very often, the worst that could happen isn't that bad. As we said before, use your logical part of your brain and work out how to solve each of your worries. It's the next step on from working out how likely it is that your worry will actually happen. Take a look at these examples.

Worry	What will happen if...	Worst case scenario AND solution
The weather keeps changing. I don't know what coat to take.	I take the wrong coat. I could get wet or hot.	I get wet or I have to carry my coat.
Someone will hurt themselves and need first aid.	I don't take a complete first aid kit?	We get a taxi to a walk-in health centre or A&E so the injured person can get the right help.

When written down, these worries seem like they aren't worries at all. Still, when an overactive brain decides that a possible scenario is a problem, it can be challenging to override it. Writing it down and working it through by thinking of the worst-case scenario often dilutes the problem and helps the brain stay calm by considering all the resources we have around us.

Having an overactive brain when it comes to anxiety can make things more challenging. However, learning how to control it and work with it can reap long-term benefits and become a tool to mitigate your anxiety surrounding certain situations before and after they happen.

CHAPTER 15

How Are You Feeling?

Answering the question, "How are you feeling?" is one of the hardest things for a person to do and autism/ADHD makes it much harder. Understanding how we feel takes a great deal of executive functioning power, and it can be hard to get a reliable answer.

When you're feeling low or maybe depressed, it can feel like your everyday normal. Being in a low mood makes it even harder to work out how you have felt at other times when you've been at your happiest.

The challenge of accurately explaining how you feel is one many people have faced. There are lots of questionnaires that medical professionals use to try and make it easier. Sometimes, questions might be confusing or complicated to understand. Maybe neurotypical people find them helpful, but autistic and ADHD people can get confused as to what the questions mean. This can make people feel worried or mixed up, which isn't helpful when you're trying to lower your anxiety.

When we need medical support, these forms have to be completed. To help you, we have written our own one, which is similar but phrased differently.

As we are all unique, having a baseline score of your

"normal" is essential. This means that somewhere, you have a record of how you feel when you're happy. This will help you spot patterns in how you feel in the long term, meaning that even if you're unsure how you feel on a particular day, you can look back at your mood pattern.

You can download these questionnaires from our website in our free downloads section in our shop or via the link below. Please fill them out regularly so you don't get worried about trying to explain how you feel. That's one type of anxiety you don't need!

Visit https://www.autability.co.uk/free-resources

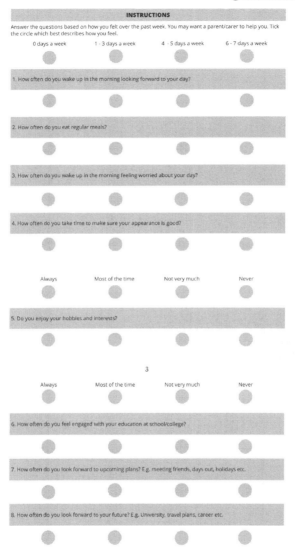

INSTRUCTIONS

Answer the questions based on how you felt over the past week. You may want a parent/carer to help you. Tick the circle which best describes how you feel.

| 0 days a week | 1 - 3 days a week | 4 - 5 days a week | 6 - 7 days a week |

1. How often do you wake up in the morning looking forward to your day?

2. How often do you eat regular meals?

3. How often do you wake up in the morning feeling worried about your day?

4. How often do you take time to make sure your appearance is good?

| Always | Most of the time | Not very much | Never |

5. Do you enjoy your hobbies and interests?

3

| Always | Most of the time | Not very much | Never |

6. How often do you feel engaged with your education at school/college?

7. How often do you look forward to upcoming plans? E.g. meeting friends, days out, holidays etc.

8. How often do you look forward to your future? E.g. University, travel plans, career etc.

Here is a section of our mood tracker. Download the whole thing for free now!

CHAPTER 16

Writing It Down

One of the most common suggestions for improving your mental health is to keep a journal of your emotions, thoughts, and feelings. This doesn't come naturally for many of us and can be challenging.

Charlotte is dyslexic as well as autistic and has ADHD. Writing, in general, and talking about her emotions are two things she can struggle with. Trying to do the two things together wouldn't help her mental health at all, and she would most likely end up writing more negative things, which doesn't help in the way the journal is supposed to. Charlotte had a counsellor once who was determined that journalling was the way to help Charlotte improve her mood and anxiety. After resisting it for quite a while, Charlotte came up with a compromise.

Instead of writing freely about how she felt, Charlotte decided on a structure to help her find the needed answers. She wrote a short list of questions to ask herself that she could answer even when feeling particularly anxious or in a very low mood. These questions made writing things down much more manageable, so she didn't try to avoid journalling anymore.

What can help autistic people is asking questions about facts, not feelings directly. Direct questions make the number of possible answers smaller, so we don't get overwhelmed trying to choose which answer fits the question the best.

If you think that this type of journaling might help you, try using the following questions and see if you find it helpful.

What could have gone better today?

Was there anything you could have done to make today go better?

Was there anything someone else could have done to make today go better?

What went well today?

Is there anything you can do to help this happen again in the future?

What are you looking forward to tomorrow?

Just because the answers to these questions will be more factual doesn't mean they won't help you process your feelings. It still helps you to see the positives happening for you despite feeling anxious and can help you pick out ways of making things better, too.

CHAPTER 17

Am I Disabled?

There are lots of different viewpoints over whether being autistic or ADHD means you have a disability. Some of you may describe yourself as being disabled already, whilst others may not, and some of you won't have ever thought about it before.

As you get older, you will become aware of ways of getting the support you need when at work or university. There are schemes like the Disabled Students Allowance, for example, which give people access to mentoring and equipment they might need whilst studying. Both Autism and ADHD, as well as other conditions like Dyslexia, are included in the list of diagnoses that qualify as a disability. For some people, the label of being disabled can make them feel very anxious.

There is no right or wrong answer as to whether you think you are disabled or not. Autism affects everyone differently, so some may say yes, they are disabled, and others may say no, they're not.

What is important to remember is that a diagnosis of autism doesn't mean you are disabled.

Whether or not autism is seen as a disability depends on the situation and the extra challenges a person might have. Often, autism is called a disability because it can make some parts of life harder, like making friends, talking to others, and doing everyday things. But autism affects everyone differently, so it doesn't always make things difficult. Sometimes, like when hanging out with friends, your autism might make things tough. Other times, like when you're doing something you love, your autism might help you do well.

We can't say whether you are disabled, but what we can help you with is anxiety surrounding disability. A hidden disability is a kind of disability that you can't see just by looking at someone. This means the person might have challenges or difficulties that aren't obvious to others. Examples include trouble with learning, feeling anxious, or having difficulty with certain social situations. Even though you can't see these disabilities, they are very real for the people who have them, and they might need extra help or understanding from others.

People with disabilities that others can't see might worry about being judged or not understood. This worry can make them feel nervous around other people. Because their disability isn't obvious, they might also be anxious about whether they'll get the help or support they need. For example, they might need to use a bathroom for disabled people and worry someone will question if they need to.

It's common for people with hidden disabilities to question themselves, wondering if their condition is real or if they're making excuses. This can make them feel anxious or like they're not good enough. This happens a lot with autism and ADHD. On days when they feel okay, they might even doubt if their symptoms are real.

You might find that how you feel can change regularly. Sometimes, knowing when you'll find everyday life easier or harder is stressful. This can make you worried about doing your tasks or joining in activities. Feeling nervous that people won't get what you're going through or won't take you seriously can make you feel anxious. Since everyone with autism and ADHD is different, it can be challenging for others to know how to help you do your best.

Whenever you feel anxious about this, remember that as long as you're honest with yourself and others about how you feel and what you struggle with, you're doing everything right. Those closest to you, as do your doctors, know what you find difficult. If you want to be able to show other people that you have a hidden disability, look online for awareness cards that you can hand out or a sunflower lanyard to help alert those who don't know you well that you might struggle, even though they can't see it.

GLOSSARY

Term	Definition
ADHD	A neurodevelopmental disorder defined by impairing levels of inattention, disorganisation, and/or hyperactivity-impulsivity. (DSM-5-TR)
Anxiety	A feeling of unease, such as worry or fear, that can be mild or severe. (www.nhs.uk)
Autism	A neurodevelopmental disorder showing significant difficulties with social communication and interaction; restricted and repetitive behaviors, interests, and activities.
Autistic/ADHD burnout	Overwhelming long-term (typically 3+ months) exhaustion, loss of function, and reduced tolerance to stimulus. (https://www.autism.org.uk/advice-and-guidance/professional-practice/autistic-burnout)

Term	Definition
DSM 5	The Diagnostic and Statistical Manual of Mental Illnesses. A guide for mental health professionals mainly in the US.
DSM 5 TR	The Diagnostic and Statistical Manual of Mental Illnesses Text Revision. Features the most current text updates based on scientific literature with contributions from more than 200 subject matter experts.
Executive functioning	Mental processes that enable us to plan, focus attention, remember, and juggle multiple tasks. (www. https:// developingchild.harvard. edu/science/key-concepts/ executive-function/)
Generalised Anxiety Disorder	Excessive anxiety and worry (apprehensive expectation), occurring more days than not for at least 6 months, about a number of events or activities. The person finds it difficult to control the worry. (DSM 5)

Term	Definition
Neurodivergent *Please note:* *Neurodivergent refers to* *many conditions and not* *just autism and ADHD.*	Differing in mental or neurological function from what is considered typical. (Oxford languages).
Neurodiversity	"Neurodiversity" is a popular term that's used to describe differences in the way people's brains work. The idea is that there's no "correct" way for the brain to work. (https://childmind.org/article/what-is-neurodiversity/)
Neurotypical	Someone who shows patterns of thought and behaviour that most people have.
Primary/Junior school	Education for 5-11 year olds
Regulate	To be able to change your state of mind so you are calm and can control your emotions and behaviours.
Safe space	A place designed specifically for someone's sensory profile where they will not be disturbed and can regulate effectively.
Secondary school	Education for 11-18 year olds

Term	Definition
Shutdown	A person will withdraw from their environment as their brain attempts to regulate and process. A person may temporarily be unable to physically move, even though they are finding the environment anxiety-inducing and stressful. (www.autability.co.uk)
Social anxiety	Persistent, intense fear or anxiety about specific social situations because you believe you may be judged negatively, embarrassed or humiliated (DSM 5)
Stimming	Also known as self stimulating behaviour, stimming is repetitive movements or noises that help an autistic person to regulate.
Transition	The change from one form, type or situation into another one.
Visual Stim	Using your eyes to engage in repetive behaviuors such as gazing or staring at things that move in a pattern (e.g. fans), staring at a light or bright colour, or blinking a lot.